Endo

"Seldom do we realize that momentary and false comforts can develop through sorrow to form a habit. Through this book, I recognized I had become subjected to re-living the pain of losing my mom for over three years. Through In Spirit, I have embraced a simple engaging way that empowers me to overcome my grieving cycles that occur on different intervals. One unforgettable experience is when I was meditating on the fruit of the Holy Spirit, a gentle breeze blew over my face and I had a vision of a huge and beautiful dog sitting beside me. The meditations in this book re-calibrated my dreams. My mom's death brought sorrow that robbed me of the gift to dream in color. I now am able to dream in beautiful colors. The book re-acquainted me to nature and to a deeper awareness of the greatness of our God. I feel this book is for all who desire a true experiential comfort with and through the Holy Spirit to overcome any subjective habitual life that feels like a heavy weight."

Cheryl Rangel, Operations Manager, India

"Tim's approach to meditation connected me to an inner voice I had long ago silenced. Through the supportive techniques that In Spirit guided me through, I was able to reconnect with the Spirit of truth within me and begin to overcome some negative thought and behavior patterns that had a stronghold on me."

Jenna Love, author
"Rajani: A Walk Toward the Light"

"In Spirit is a gift that links my meditations with the use of nature. A more empowering form of prayer opened up to me when In Spirit walked me outdoors for some of the practices. In Spirit is a valuable and constructive tool. Its contemplations and practices help empower one to break negative routines and establish beneficial ones."

Charlotte Smith, Spiritual Director, Poet
"A Transplanted Soul"

"All of us tend to escape the present moment. We abandon our own selves in the hope that we can find life in externals. This book reminds us where life is: in our spirits, hearts, and minds. *In Spirit* there is no other place of true life."

Leslie Cole, M.D.
Cedar Recovery in Mt. Juliet, TN

"With 45 years of experience of leading people to healing joy of living fully, I recommend *In Spirit* as a place to begin practicing living life in the present. With love through the dynamic experiential presence of God, one encounters God on all levels of their personality: head, heart and gut. I know Tim personally and he has the authority to coach the practice of experiencing God because he lives it. These practices will move you from darkness to light."

Dr. Terry Sanford Smith, Life Coach, Author
"Delta Blues - From Darkness to Light"

IN SPIRIT

A 28-DAY JUMP-START
TO LIVE BY THE SPIRIT

TIM MEHTA

IN SPIRIT RHYTHM, LLC

Published in Nashville, Tennessee, by In Spirit Rhythm, LLC

inspiritrhythm@gmail.com

www.inspiritrhythm.com

Book art design by Tim Mehta.

Scripture quotations marked NIV are taken from the THE HOLY BIBLE, NEW INTERNATIONAL VERSION®, NIV® Copyright © 1973, 1978, 1984, 2011 by Biblica, Inc.® Used by permission. All rights reserved worldwide. Scripture quotations marked NASB are taken from the NEW AMERICAN STANDARD BIBLE®, Copyright © 1960, 1962, 1963, 1968, 1971, 1972, 1973, 1975, 1977, 1995 by The Lockman Foundation. Used by permission. Scripture quotation marked NLT are taken from the Holy Bible, New Living Translation, copyright © 1996, 2004, 2007 by Tyndale House Foundation. Used by permission of Tyndale House Publishers, Inc., Carol Stream, Illinois 60188. All rights reserved.

ISBN-10: 1534754148
ISBN-13: 978-1534754140

"We proclaim to you what we have seen and heard, so that you also may have fellowship with us. And our fellowship is with the Father and with His Son, Jesus Christ. We write this to make our joy complete." (1 John 1:3-4 NIV)

"This is how we know that we live in Him and He in us: He has given us of His Spirit." (1 John 4:13 NIV)

CONTENTS

A Note from the Author

The practice of being *in Spirit* with Jesus fosters many personal transformations. Foremost, it creates a new perspective toward the life we have been living and the renewed life we begin to experience. It also generates new, higher thoughts, and healthier emotional patterns. Overall, *in Spirit* living brings forth tangible results that steer our life in a positive direction, enhancing our spiritual sense.

I often reflect on the day I fell to my knees in despair, believing life was a worthless effort. My soul was filled with destructive thoughts and feelings. I felt powerless to attain a state of peace. I felt powerless to change anything in my being. My mind judged my heart, and my heart hated the way I thought. It was as if there was a war within me. I remember saying, "Lord, I cannot live the life You are calling me to live. I desire to die. But I am giving You this chance to intervene. If You want Your will for my life to be seen in me, You are going to have to do it. Therefore, Lord, I give You my body as a living sacrifice, holy and blameless, not because of anything I have done, but because of everything You have done, through the body and blood of Jesus. Thank You, Father, for loving me so deeply. Come live in and live through me. Fill me with Your Spirit. May I feel the fruit of Your Spirit: love, joy, peace, patience, kindness, goodness, faithfulness, gentleness and self-control. In Jesus Name, AMEN."

After that despairing moment, I began to pray daily, upon waking, using the prayer above as a template.

Throughout each day, I attempted to walk in mindfulness, with the awareness that my core self was deeply connected to Spirit in a way I had never before been able to perceive. I was aware of a stronger, more powerful spiritual life-form—JESUS—living within my body. The new experience was monumental. The One who has mastery over all other spirits, including my own, chooses to live in me and through me.

I still live with imperfections, but I now have a renewed sense of self-love. As I live *in Spirit*, I attempt to keep my focus on Jesus, understanding that He is real, He lives, and His promises are for everyone. He pursues, He chases, and He loves like a groom in pursuit of his bride.

Transformation can occur within anyone. There is nothing we have done or could do that has the power to separate us from God's love. If we are entangled in an addiction, His love is steady. If we are pulled astray by lustful desire, His love is unwavering. If we are harming our self or another person, His love is steadfast. We can count on God's enduring love.

Inner transformation requires patience, and patience requires mercy. Mercy towards self is necessary for the rough days when we feel we might have a setback or face a difficult day. The truth, through spiritual wisdom and understanding, continually sets me free from any negative bondage or hateful thought that is formed in my mind against self and towards others.

If you are in a place similar to the one I was in—feeling paralyzed by your inability to climb out of the darkness and becoming unrecognizable to yourself—it's OKAY! God, through His Spirit, took me where I was and accepted me. His kindness and His unfailing, unconditional love empowered me to gradually put my total trust in Him. The discipline of being *in Spirit* has recalibrated my spiritual wiring and given me a new better understanding of trust and surrender.

As you journey through your transformation, be prepared for your mind and heart to go through a metamorphosis—a time of darkness before the light of a new birth. This occurs in His timing, as one engages Jesus *in Spirit*. It only takes a seed-sized amount of faith to begin. Your restored faith will become more evident as you experience the power that comes by being in Spirit.

Throughout this book, "in Spirit" is used interchangeably in reference to in Father, in Jesus, in Holy Spirit, and in our own spirit. In our own spirit because it is through our own spirit we receive an open invitation to fellowship as one with God *in Spirit*.

Introduction

The intent of *In Spirit* is to provide a 28-day jump-start to live by the Spirit for those seeking to discover or improve their own spiritual walk. *In Spirit* is a compilation of Contemplations, Practices, and Reflections (CPR's). The 28 CPR's are rooted in the teachings of Jesus and His apostles, Old Testament examples, and my personal experience in overcoming addiction and standing up under temptation.

Contemplations are to draw attention to supposed realities from a spiritual angle, challenging the mind. **Practices** give opportunity for the heart to feel the reality and then aid the mind and heart to live together. Compared to breathing, practices would be *inhaling*, while reflections would be *exhaling*. **Reflections** are times for recording, journaling, and personal dialogue. This means allowing time for the heart and mind to have a conversation. Allow the heart to express while the mind listens. Allow the mind and heart to reason through new thought and new feeling.

Jesus Christ helps me to see who I truly am as a human being. His life on earth was a brilliant display of a human's potential in fellowship with their Creator. He is a true friend, loving His friends even as they deserted Him. He is a pursuer, a jealous lover, and a compassionate brother. Through intentionally engaging Christ *in Spirit*, I am growing to know this about Him.

Being *in Spirit* is a way to come to know a God that loves you even at your worst. It is a way to understand self and then, with God's Spirit, begin to live a life with an inward feeling of His eternal presence.

Go at your own pace. It may be easy for the mind to gather knowledge, but the heart may need time to process the new feelings. Follow through with the practices. Repeat them as often as you would like. Some thoughts you may accept and integrate, others you may not. Explore the thoughts presented. Seek opposing viewpoints. Ask questions to a variety of people . . . then seek answers that resonate with the truth of the Spirit.

Humans are complex creatures who are able to influence and be influenced in a variety of ways. Understanding the different ways takes time. Positive change normally does not happen overnight.

In my darkest moment I contemplated suicide. Though I began to experience freedom and healing shortly afterward, I still traveled through about three months of suffering as old thought and emotional patterns tried to maintain their mastery over me. Sometimes I gave in; however, I kept giving myself over to being *in Spirit*, feeling unworthy or worthless at times. His words, "Never will I leave you, never will I forsake you" are true. Today, I am still on a journey of coming to know Jesus and feeling more free than I did during those initial days.

I began *in Spirit* as a private practice of being silent for three minutes. It then grew to encompass many things, including a weekly gathering with men and women (my spiritual brothers and sisters) who desire to commune with the Lord through the breaking of the bread and drinking of the wine. Together, we seek to know Christ and His power as He lives and works among us. We openly and honestly share our personal life experiences. This interaction is a wondrous experience where one can hear, and sometimes witness, Christ transforming and healing others through the Spirit.

May the gracious God and Father of our Lord Jesus Christ grant you grace and peace with hope of a new life in fellowship with Him. Amen.

DAYS 1 THROUGH 7

BEING HUMAN
THE BODY
THE MIND
THE HEART
THE SPIRIT
IN THE IMAGE OF ADAM
HUMAN NATURE

BEFORE YOU BEGIN DAY 1…

Physically, we are born into our earthly environment in bodies with the ability to absorb through our senses. Our senses (seeing, hearing, touching, etc…) pick up on "energies" in the environment, and then we, in turn, absorb these "energies" into our body. These absorptions influence our thought and emotional patterns and are the initial shapers of our mind and heart.

Spiritual birth gives us a spiritual sense so that being *in Spirit* also becomes a shaper influencing our thought and emotional patterns. This begins the process of renewing the mind and purifying the heart. Being *in Spirit* gives new perspectives with wisdom and understanding giving life new meaning.

The first week of CPR's is designed to establish a foundational view of what it means to be human. It then begins to build upon this foundation with understanding of the body, mind, heart, and spirit. Once these are well acquainted, it discusses comforts that we receive through our mortal bodies as well as through our human nature.

Set your own pace. There is no need to rush. It is OKAY to take each day a week at a time.

If you choose to contemplate and practice in the morning, then reflect throughout the day. Record your reflections at the end of the day. This way there is time to absorb and react to any new experiences, thoughts, or feelings.

DAY 1 - BEING HUMAN

CONTEMPLATION

Being a human, you have a body, a mind, a heart, and a spirit. Your body is from the earth. It is a temporary vessel through which you interact. Your body is dependant on many things to live.

Your spirit is a breath of God. Your spirit is an eternal unseen presence. The true essence of you is spirit.

Your mind and heart, together, comprise your soul. Your mind is a place of thought and reason. Your heart is a place of emotion and feeling. Your soul (mind and heart) is very vulnerable, yet powerful. Without your soul (mind and heart), the essence of you (spirit) could never fully communicate with others through your body.

PRACTICE

Find a comfortable quiet place.

Take at least three minutes to be still.
(Be still means to bring the body to a still position and focus on breathing)

Focus on breathing.

Acknowledge the components of being human
(body, heart, mind, and spirit).

Focus on being spirit.

Voice: "I am spirit. I am a breath of God"
(repeat three times)

As spirit, bring your thoughts to your heart. Allow your mind to acknowledge your heart.

Voice: "I have a heart, I am capable of feeling. With all my mind, I will care for my heart."
(repeat three times)

PRACTICE

As spirit, bring your emotions to your mind. Allow the heart to acknowledge your mind.

Voice: "I have a mind, I am capable of processing thoughts. With all my heart, I love my mind."
(repeat three times)

As spirit, move through your soul (heart and mind), and acknowledge your body.

Voice: "I have a body. It is of the earth. It is dependant on many things. With my all my soul, I will care for my body."
(repeat three times)

REFLECTION

Give yourself time to reflect through the day. If you choose, write or draw any reflections you experienced. Explore creativity, perhaps even recording your voice in words or song. This is to allow time for your heart and mind to have a conversation. Allow your heart to feel while your mind listens. Allow your mind to reason while in tune with your heart. When your heart senses freedom, call forth a word, a picture, a description, or a story that captures the truth that enabled that feeling of freedom.

REFLECTION

DAY 2 - THE BODY

CONTEMPLATION

Your body is from the earth. It is a temporary vessel through which you interact. Your body is dependant on many things to live. Your body needs you (spirit), blood, air, water, warmth, and food to live. Naturally, we will feel physical discomfort if any of these needs are not supplied within a given amount of time. Caring for your body is important.

Your body interacts with the world through its senses. The five senses are: hearing, seeing, touching, smelling, and tasting. The ability of these senses can vary from one individual to another. For example, one who lacks the ability to see may have enhanced abilities of the other four. Even if one has all five senses, the abilities of the senses can be enhanced.

In Spirit living often activates the senses of the body. The miracles of Jesus consisted of restoring peoples' use of their senses. He restored the eyes of the blind, the legs of the lame, the hands of the lepers, and the ears of the deaf (Matthew 11:1-6).

Jesus referred to the use of the senses in His teachings. "Look at the birds of the air; they do not sow or reap or store away in barns, and yet your heavenly Father feeds them. Are you not much more valuable than they?" (Matthew 6:26 NIV). "See how the flowers of the field grow. They do not labor or spin" (Matthew 6:28 NIV). "The wind blows wherever it pleases. You hear its sound, but you cannot tell where it comes from or where it is going. So it is with everyone born of the Spirit" (John 3:5-8 NIV). Considering the details of what we hear, see, touch, smell, and taste can give awareness, releasing tension within the body and soul.

I haven't always been happy with my body. When I was a teenager, I remember standing in front of a mirror focusing on all the flaws of my body. I felt ashamed of some of the things I noticed. Often it would affect my self-esteem making myself feel less when around others.

Later, as I became a young adult, I began going to the gym regularly and began receiving compliments on my look. This felt good. But over time I began to notice that when I didn't get a look or receive a compliment, my self-esteem was affected.

In Spirit living assures me that I am not my body and even if my body has so called "flaws"… it's OKAY! There are still much more things about my body to appreciate and that with, I can experience life. My self-esteem does not have to be dependent on the way my body is or looks, through my eyes or the eyes of others.

PRACTICE

Find a place to experience nature in a park, garden, or backyard.

Find a comfortable quiet place.

Take at least three minutes to be still.

Focus on breathing.

Acknowledge the senses of the body: hearing, seeing, touching, smelling, and tasting.

Focus on hearing. Open the mind and heart to listen.

Focus on seeing. Open the mind and heart to watch.

Focus on touching. Open the mind and heart to feel.

Focus on smelling. Open the mind and heart to breathe.

Focus on tasting. Open the mind and heart to receive.

Acknowledge the body and the use of its senses.

Voice: "I have a body. It is of the earth. It is dependant on many things. With all my soul, I will care for my body."
(repeat three times)

PRACTICE

Throughout your day:

Breathe, giving thanks for the free gift of air.

Drink water, giving thanks for the refreshment.

Feel the climate, giving thanks for the protection.

Eat food, giving thanks for the color, tastes, and smells.

REFLECTION

Give yourself time to reflect through the day. If you choose, write or draw any reflections you experienced. Explore creativity, perhaps even recording your voice in words or song. This is to allow time for your heart and mind to have a conversation. Allow your heart to feel while your mind listens. Allow your mind to reason while in tune with your heart. When your heart senses freedom, call forth a word, a picture, a description, or a story that captures the truth that enabled that feeling of freedom.

REFLECTION

REFLECTION

DAY 3 - THE MIND

CONTEMPLATION

Your mind and heart, together, comprise your soul. Your mind is a place of thought and reason. Your heart is a place of emotion and feeling. Your soul (mind and heart) is very vulnerable, yet powerful. Without your soul, the essence of you (spirit) could never fully communicate with others through your body.

Your mind is a gift, with several capabilities. Your mind can consider, contemplate, determine, focus, reason, record, remember, think, etc. Many of us use our minds to protect ourselves from physical or emotional harm, attempting to control circumstances. However, mental strain can often be felt with the use of mind control.

Governing the mind can reduce or eliminate mental strain. Being *in Spirit* will aid in the governing of the mind. A mind governed by the Spirit feels less stressful.

Mark 5:1-20 describes an extreme case where a man is completely "out of his mind." Through this story we see that the mind of this man became subjected to more powerful sources that governed his mind to do things he would not normally do.

With me it was not to such an extreme. At least, I do not think so. I had many past experiences, including my perspective in those moments, governing my mind. This was affecting the way I thought and reasoned. This

37

caused my heart to feel anger, hate, envy, jealousy, and self-pity. It also caused my heart, at times, to become prideful, which led to arrogance, gloating, perfectionism, and the felt need to hide my failures for fear of being judged.

I know I am not alone, but even if I were… it's OKAY! The power that I continue to feel from being *in Spirit* is giving me a renewed way to reason through loving self and others. It is a wonderful and beautiful experience.

PRACTICE

Read Mark 5:1-20.

Look up the following verses and consider the mind and its function:

Psalm 1:2:

> The mind participates in meditation.

Psalm 4:4:

> The mind can search the heart and be silent.

Proverbs 12:5:

> The mind can make plans.
> The mind can give deceitful advice.

Proverbs 15:26:

> The mind can have wicked thoughts.

PRACTICE

Find a comfortable quiet place.

Take at least three minutes to be still.

Focus on breathing.

Acknowledge the mind and its importance.

Embrace the gift of the mind and accept the ability to think, reason, and ponder.

Voice: "I have a mind, I am capable of processing thoughts. With all my heart, I love my mind."
(repeat three times)

As an ongoing practice:

Search the words *mind, thought,* and *think* within the book of Psalms and Proverbs. Make a list of words that help describe the mind and its function.

REFLECTION

Give yourself time to reflect throughout the day. If you choose, write or draw any reflections you experienced. Explore creativity, perhaps even recording your voice in words or song. This is to allow time for your heart and mind to have a conversation. Allow your heart to feel while your mind listens. Allow your mind to reason while in tune with your heart. When your heart senses freedom, call forth a word, a picture, a description, or a story that captures the truth that enabled that feeling of freedom.

REFLECTION

REFLECTION

DAY 4 - THE HEART

CONTEMPLATION

Your mind and heart, together, comprise your soul. Your mind is a place of thought and reason. Your heart is a place of emotion and feeling. Your soul (mind and heart) is very vulnerable, yet powerful. Without your soul, the essence of you (spirit) could never fully communicate with others through your body.

From your heart come desire and passion. These contribute to will, drive, pursuit, endurance, perseverance, and character. Your heart is the powerhouse of your soul. It is very important to care for and condition your heart.

Being *in Spirit* conditions the heart with fruit of the Spirit: love, joy, peace, patience, kindness, goodness, faithfulness, gentleness, and self-control (which I like to call spirit-control because spirit is our true self). The more we exercise being *in Spirit*, the more positive energy we receive to face our fears. We *can* taste the fruit of the Spirit in the midst of our challenges.

The story found in Mark 4:35-41 illustrates how a trial can reveal the true condition of the soul. In this story we can understand that fear combined with a lack of faith can lead us to irrational thinking, judgments, and guilt. These men's hearts had not yet been conditioned to believe the power in Jesus' words. Instead, they saw the storm . . . and they felt the storm. They desired (of the heart) to stay alive. They acted on what they knew (of the mind) to stay alive . . . and persevered (of the heart) to stay alive. Their minds and hearts were in a struggle. As a result, their will could not be obtained so they panicked and questioned Jesus and His love for them.

I have questioned God and His love for me, and… it's OKAY! It is quite natural for man to do this, and it is part of the process of growing *in Spirit*. There are many aspects of my life I did not ask for which affected the way I experienced life. Some experiences I dreamt of having will never happen, and… it's OKAY! Because *in Spirit* experiences I have had, and continue to have, are beyond what I could ever ask or dream. I find them much more fitting and joyful. But before these *in Spirit* experiences occurred, I was in a place of questioning.

So many times I have been in this boat, repeating this story, and every time hearing, "Peace, be still." Will I ever be in a place where I don't question? I might hope so, but one thing I have learned is that at the end of every repeated story is a voice saying, "Peace, be still." This gives rest to my mind and comfort to my heart.

PRACTICE

Read Mark 4:35-41.

Imagine yourself with your family or close friends in this story as the disciples.

Take a few moments to describe how your minds and your hearts would interact with each other.

Consider other real-life struggles that involve desperation, time crunches, panic, and poor judgment.

Describe the interaction between the mind and heart in these real life struggles.

Look up the following verses and consider the heart and its function:

Psalm 10:17:

> The heart can produce desire, can feel affliction and encouragement, and can cry.

Proverbs 12:25:

> The heart can be weighed down with anxiety, but with one kind word can feel cheer.

PRACTICE

Find a comfortable quiet place.

Be still for at least three minutes. Focus on breathing.

Acknowledge the heart and its importance.

Embrace the gift of the heart and accept the ability to feel.

Voice: "I have a heart, I am capable of feeling. With all my mind, I will care for my heart."
(repeat three times)

As an ongoing practice:

Search the word *heart*, *desire*, and *passion* throughout Psalms and Proverbs. Make a list of words that help describe the heart and its function.

REFLECTION

Give yourself time to reflect through the day. If you choose, write or draw any reflections you experienced. Explore creativity, perhaps even recording your voice in words or song. This is to allow time for your heart and mind to have a conversation. Allow your heart to feel while your mind listens. Allow your mind to reason while in tune with your heart. When your heart senses freedom, call forth a word, a picture, a description, or a story that captures the truth that enabled that feeling of freedom.

REFLECTION

REFLECTION

DAY 5 - THE SPIRIT

CONTEMPLATION

Your spirit is a breath of God. Your spirit is an eternal unseen presence. The true essence of you is spirit.

Being *in Spirit* is a practice of spiritual fellowship with the Father, the Son, Holy Spirit, and with each other. Through this spiritual fellowship, God comforts the soul by governing the mind and conditioning the heart. Without spiritual fellowship, the soul can lack this comfort. Without comfort from the Spirit through spiritual fellowship, the soul will feel discomfort and will seek comfort through the body.

1 Samuel 8 begins our introduction to Israel's first human king, Saul. He is from the smallest tribe of the twelve tribes of Israel. Samuel is Israel's judge at the time when the people are requesting a king. The Lord chooses Saul as king and Samuel anoints him king over Israel.

Saul begins his reign with the anointing of the Lord. Saul's initial response appears to be from a state of humility, or, possibly, low self-esteem. Under pressure as king, Saul acts foolishly by offering up a sacrifice that he is not to offer. Samuel rebukes him for his actions. Saul does not respond with a repentant heart seeking the comfort (fellowship) of the Spirit. He continues his duties as king but does not act according to the word of the Lord spoken through Samuel; therefore the Lord regrets making Saul king. The Lord informs Samuel that

Saul has turned away from the Lord (1 Sam. 15:10). In other words, Saul stopped being *in Spirit; therefore* his spiritual fellowship with the Lord was non-existent. Though he still acted religiously, he lacked spiritual fellowship through *in-Spirit* living.

Samuel tells Saul that the Lord has rejected him as king. This causes Saul to confess his sin for violating the word of the Lord. However, they are only words with no actions of humility. The words of the Lord to Saul through Samuel are meant to humble Saul, but Saul never humbles himself. Over time, the Lord anoints David, son of Jesse, as king over Israel through Samuel.

When the Spirit of the Lord departs from Saul, an evil spirit begins to torment him (1 Samuel 16:14). With no spiritual fellowship, Saul feels torment (discomfort), and his friends encourage him to seek out someone who can play the lyre to provide comfort through music. They search for a lyre player and discover David can play for Saul.

As David wins battles and receives praise by the people for his accomplishments, Saul is filled with jealousy to the point of desiring to murder David. With the lack of spiritual comfort, Saul seeks out comfort through his body by enjoying the sound of the lyre and receiving praise from others. When David interferes with Saul receiving these comforts, Saul's mind and heart conspires to put David to death.

Let me say this: I know what it feels like to be Saul! I have thoughts that pass through my mind that are against myself and/or others. This occurs when I find myself comparing myself to other people. If I allow myself to continue to meditate on what I don't have, judgmental and hateful thoughts usually take root and grow in my mind. This impacts my heart and my connection with others. Continually meditating on what I don't have impacts my relationships in a negative way.

Being *in Spirit* trains me to be thankful for the little things that I do have and experience. Giving thanks is powerful because it draws my focus toward how my life is truly and uniquely blessed in the little things. Being *in Spirit* has taught me that sometimes I'm last, and... it's OKAY!

PRACTICE

Being *in Spirit* gives access to experience spiritual fellowship with the Father, Christ, and Holy Spirit.

Being *in Spirit,* allows you, as spirit, to embrace the anointing of the Lord.

Listen: "Now it is God who makes both us and you stand firm in Christ. He anointed us, set His seal of ownership on us, and put His Spirit in our hearts as a deposit, guaranteeing what is to come." (2 Corinthians 1:21-22 NIV)

Look up the following verses and consider the anointing of the Lord and the spirit:

Psalm 18:50:

> The anointed can see unfailing love.

Psalm 84:9:

> The anointed has God's favor.

Proverbs 1:23:

> Through the spirit, wisdom pours out thoughts and teachings.

Proverbs 15:4:

> A perverse tongue can crush the spirit.

PRACTICE

Find a comfortable, quite place.

Be still for at least three minutes. Focus on breathing.

Voice: "I am spirit. I am a breath of God."
(repeat three times)

Allow the anointing of the Holy Spirit, Jesus, and the Father to pour like oil upon your head. Slowly allow that flow of oil, the anointing, and the Spirit to completely cover you.

Imagine God breathing.

God breathes in (you are in Him).

God breathes out (He is in you).

Voice: "I am a breath of God."
(repeat three times)

Focus on your own breathing.

Breathe in (He is in you).

Breathe out (you are in Him).

Voice: "God's presence is in the air I breathe"
(repeat three times)

PRACTICE

Jesus compares the Spirit to living water, and wind.

Today, observe and be attentive to water and wind.

Voice: "I am spirit. I am a breath of God"
(repeat three times)

Voice: "God is present as Spirit. This is the air I breathe and the water I drink."
(repeat three times)

As on ongoing practice:

Search for and meditate on the words *spirit*, *anointed*, and *anointing* in Psalms and Proverbs. Make a list of words that describe the anointing of the Lord.

REFLECTION

Give yourself time to reflect through the day. If you choose, write or draw any reflections you experienced. Explore creativity, perhaps even recording your voice in words or song. This is to allow time for your heart and mind to have a conversation. Allow your heart to feel while your mind listens. Allow your mind to reason while in tune with your heart. When your heart senses freedom, call forth a word, a picture, a description, or a story that captures the truth that enabled that feeling of freedom.

REFLECTION

REFLECTION

DAY 6 - IN THE IMAGE OF ADAM

CONTEMPLATION

Adam and Eve were created in the Image of God as it is written, "Let Us make man in Our Image, in Our likeness ..." (Genesis 1:26 NIV). But after the initial sin and being cast out of the Garden of Eden, Seth is born and this is what is written:

> "When God created man, He made him in the likeness of God. He created them male and female and blessed them. And when they were created, He called them "man." When Adam had lived 130 years, he had a son *in his own likeness, in his own image,* and he named him Seth." (Gen. 5:1-3 NIV)

Our bodies are in the image of Adam, the way he and his wife became after the initial sin. By acknowledging the image of Adam, we will not put so much confidence in our bodies, realizing their fragility. Our bodies are limited. The sensations of comfort the soul can feel through the body are limited and fade over time.

An addiction is when the soul is constantly using the body to provide a limiting and fading comfort, and is seeking to make it ongoing (eternal). If you are aware of an uncontrollable activity in your life that is hurting you and/or others, believe that this activity does not have power over you. Being *in Spirit* daily provides access to eternal comfort to empower the soul to break the endless cycles. You will discover wisdom and understanding, bringing joy and peace to your soul.

I remember when I was controlled by certain activities. I remember the luring affect they had over me and on me in thought and feeling. I remember losing my battles and becoming my own battle. I remember feeling desperate and helpless. I remember feeling stuck. I remember the guilt. I remember days feeling eternally dark. I remember the agony of my soul and my cry for help.

All of these emotions are common to us who encounter activities that master our souls. None of us are alone. These emotions are but a part of a birth process of a new *in Spirit* life so… it's OKAY!

Overcoming my addictions was not easy. At times I felt crazy, alone, terrified, miserable . . . and I hated life. However, as I faced each day, one day at a time, and faced each hour of each day, one hour at a time, being *in Spirit* gave me the assurance that even through this… I am OKAY!

Yes, I had hard battles that I fought, but I became more masterful in self-control and perseverance through each battle, even though I felt I had lost. This prepared me for the next battle. Eventually, I began to have some victories. As I grew *in Spirit*, I began to understand much more about our human experience and began to hear truth of whose I truly am. This is when I began to feel freedom.

PRACTICE

Write down any addiction you are aware of in your life on a piece of paper.

Find a comfortable quiet place.

Be still for at least three minutes. Focus on breathing.

Read Matthew 6:9-13.

Voice the "Lord's prayer" slowly, reflecting on the depth of each word.

Now Voice:

"Our Father, who dwells in the unseen,
how great is Your Name.
Your reign come within me.
Your will be done in our spirits as it is in Your Spirit,
in our hearts as it is in Your heart,
in our minds as it is in Your mind.
Give us today nourishment for our bodies.
Have mercy on us as we are merciful towards others.
Shepherd us to stand up under every temptation.
Allow us to experience Your power in deliverance from
evil. For Yours is the kingdom and the power
and the glory forever and ever. AMEN."
(repeat three times)

Take the paper on which you wrote your addictions and burn it.

PRACTICE

Begin practicing self-control and perseverance on any issue or area in which you find easier to control *in Spirit*.

Perhaps, begin some form of daily physical exercise.

This can first be a spiritual exercise of the spirit, then the physical body.

Listen to the body, but give power to the spirit to master the body rather than the body mastering the spirit.

REFLECTION

Give yourself time to reflect through the day. If you choose, write or draw any reflections you experienced. Explore creativity, perhaps even recording your voice in words or song. This is to allow time for your heart and mind to have a conversation. Allow your heart to feel while your mind listens. Allow your mind to reason while in tune with your heart. When your heart senses freedom, call forth a word, a picture, a description, or a story that captures the truth that enabled that feeling of freedom.

REFLECTION

REFLECTION

DAY 7 - THE HUMAN NATURE

CONTEMPLATION

Have you ever compared yourself with someone else? How do you feel when you judge that someone is more superior to you? How do you feel when you judge that you are more superior to another?

Valued, secure, in control, proud, important, and arrogant are often what we feel when we think we are superior. Jealous, envious, covetous, resentful and powerless is often what we feel when we think another is superior. Instead of focusing on these feelings, let's ask the question, Why is it in our human nature to compare ourselves to others?

To be labeled less-than feels powerless. In this place of feeling less-than, we see ourselves as unnecessary, unwanted, unrecognized, and even without significant talent. However, superiority is enticing because it creates a powerful feeling, a feeling of belonging and worthiness that attracts attention and praise. Which place fills the soul with comfort? To be superior gives this comfort.

Winning feels better than losing. So, if we are not the greatest, we at least want to be on the winning team. This leads us to compare groups—us verses them. But within the team, we place ourselves in comparison with each other. We do this to feel comfort.

Eternal comfort (rest) that our souls so desperately

need cannot be obtained through the body. When our spirits begin to understand this about our souls and bodies, we encounter a "poor in spirit" state.

It was a breakthrough for me when I realized that all I need is comfort. This meant my sinful life was not because I was evil but that I had a need which was not being filled in a healthy way and... I was OKAY!

As I was listening to the scriptures in 2 Corinthians, I heard that "God was a God of all comfort, who comforts us in all our troubles" (2 Corinthians 1:3-4 NIV). I began to wonder how God could comfort me in the midst of my discomforts.

As I was listening to the scriptures in Luke, I heard after being baptized, Jesus was filled with the Holy Spirit and the Spirit led Jesus in the wilderness being tempted by the devil. After His wilderness time, Jesus came out in power of the Spirit (compare Luke 4:1 with 4:14). He was filled with the Spirit entering the wilderness, then, He was empowered by the Spirit leaving the wilderness. My thoughts centered on this empowerment. What happened to Jesus to allow Him to be in this power? He was tempted, and by the comfort of the Holy Spirit, Jesus overcame the temptations.

I began to face my temptations, and in the midst of my temptations, I would voice: "Father, give me the comfort that I am seeking that only you can provide: The comfort of love, joy peace, patience, kindness, goodness, faithfulness, gentleness, and self-control." I then would feel inner peace flow through my being.

PRACTICE

The Sermon on the Mount found in Matthew 5:3-12 begins with the "poor in spirit" state of consciousness.

The beatitudes is not something we focus on in an attempt to perform, but rather they represent a way the Spirit of God moves in our lives to transform us to reflect the ministry of Jesus (from His baptism to His resurrection, Acts 1:21-22). Each reflection comes in an individual, special, and unique way.

A daily *in Spirit* practice acknowledges this flow and surrenders any human nature resisting this flow to take place. As we begin to experience this in our own lives, we indirectly become grounded in our faith. We will transition from trying to believe because what is written, to believing because our experiences confirm what is written.

PRACTICE

Read Matthew 5:3-12, and consider the following:

"poor in spirit":   our spirits lack what it takes to live the utmost life relying solely on our souls and bodies

"those who mourn":   the crying of our souls and spirits for eternal comfort

"the meek":   our attitude of humility and our willingness to be taught

"those who hunger and
thirst for righteousness":   our longing for God's favor and His Spirit

"the merciful":   our outward expressions of our inward experience in the Spirit

PRACTICE

"the pure in heart": those whose hearts are comforted and conditioned by the Spirit

"the peacemakers": those whose minds are comforted and governed by the Spirit

"those who are persecuted": the inward withdrawals of the human sinful nature as the Spirit begins to govern

"are you when people insult": the outward insults from religious and non-religious people

PRACTICE

Find a comfortable quiet place.

Be still for at least three minutes. Focus on breathing.

Acknowledge weaknesses of your human nature.

Give your body, mind, heart, and spirit to the Spirit of God.

Voice: "I give You my body as a living sacrifice. I give You my mind to govern. I give You my heart to condition. I give You my spirit to comfort with Your anointing. In the Name of Jesus, AMEN"
(repeat three times)

Give additional time in prayer, voicing any thoughts and/or feelings.

REFLECTION

Give yourself time to reflect through the day. If you choose, write or draw any reflections you experienced. Explore creativity, perhaps even recording your voice in words or song. This is to allow time for your heart and mind to have a conversation. Allow your heart to feel while your mind listens. Allow your mind to reason while in tune with your heart. When your heart senses freedom, call forth a word, a picture, a description, or a story that captures the truth that enabled that feeling of freedom.

REFLECTION

REFLECTION

DAYS 8 THROUGH 14

SOUND AND LIGHT
SEPARATION
A SEED
GOVERN
MULTIPLY
IN THE IMAGE OF GOD
REST

BEFORE YOU BEGIN DAY 8...

The apostle Paul wrote to the Romans explaining that by understanding from what has been made, people are able to see God's invisible qualities, which are His eternal power and divine nature (Romans 1:20).

The next seven days we focus on the first seven days of history, when God created the heavens and the earth. Understanding how God created everything outside of us offers a fresh perspective on how He chooses to create within us. Each day we take what we can see outside ourselves and internalize it. We will grow to understand how we can experience God's divine nature and eternal power in our lives.

Again, go at your own pace. These contemplations and practices will take additional time. Also, give time before recording any reflections.

DAY 8 - SOUND AND LIGHT

CONTEMPLATION

"In the beginning God created the heavens and the earth. Now the earth was formless and empty, darkness was over the surface of the deep, and the Spirit of God was hovering over the waters. And God said, "Let there be light," and there was light. God saw that the light was good, and He separated the light from the darkness. God called the light "day," and the darkness He called "night." And there was evening, and there was morning—the first day. (Genesis 1:1-5 NIV)

On day one there is the sound of God voicing light. Sound and light are forms of energy that produce vibrations. Vibrations affect the body, heart, mind, and spirit.

Thoughts and feelings can be considered as vibrations of energy. If both the mind and heart are independently producing vibration, then it is important that they both be in sync or in harmony. If the mind and heart are out of sync with each other, then we feel an internal discomfort.

When we see an object, we are actually seeing how the object reflects light. Light, and the way it reflects, has the ability to control thought and feeling. Walking into a white-walled room produces different thoughts and feelings compared to walking into a room with walls painted black.

Likewise, sound has the ability to control thought and feeling. When we hear a sound, the tone can strike a feeling of peace or of fear. Sound can trigger the body to have chills, to sweat, or to quiver.

In Spirit, we experience the light of Christ. Through Christ, for Christ, and by Christ all things were created and made; therefore we give Him the time to tune our minds and hearts to vibrate in harmony with His. This allows Him to shine His light into our hearts.

"For God, who said, 'Let light shine out of darkness,' made His light shine in our hearts to give us the light of the knowledge of God's glory displayed in the face of Christ." (2 Corinthians 4:6 NIV)

"You are my hiding place; You will protect me from trouble and surround me with songs of deliverance." (Psalm 32:7 NIV)

PRACTICE

What colors bring you comfort?

What sounds make your feel peace?

As an ongoing practice, you may desire to create a space using these chosen colors and sounds as a place to reflect. Jesus found such a place in a garden.

Feel free to create a sacred meditation space for yourself. Be creative in the use of sounds and light. Over time, this space can adapt and change as you experience change.

Being *in Spirit* allows us to grow to know Christ and His power. What we experience through what we see with our eyes, hear with our ears, and touch with our hands are shadows of the unseen. We can use the shadows to condition the eyes and ears of the heart to experience the reality of the unseen.

PRACTICE

Find a comfortable quiet place to be still.

Be still for at least three minutes. Focus on breathing.

Listen: "For God, who said, 'Let light shine out of darkness,' made His light shine in our hearts to give us the light of the knowledge of God's glory displayed in the face of Christ." (2 Corinthians 4:6 NIV)

Voice: "Father, may the light You shine in my heart open the eyes of my heart to know and experience Your glory."
(repeat three times)

Be still for at least three minutes allowing Jesus to fill you with His light.

Continue when you are ready.

Listen: "You are my hiding place; You will protect me from trouble and surround me with songs of deliverance." (Psalm 32:7 NIV)

Voice: "Father, may the song of deliverance You sing over me tune my soul to be in harmony with You."
(repeat three times)

Allow time for your soul to be tuned.

Stay in a quiet state for as long as you would like.

REFLECTION

Give yourself time to reflect through the day. If you choose write or draw any reflections you experienced. Explore creativity, perhaps even recording your voice in words or song. This is to allow time for your heart and mind to have a conversation. Allow your heart to feel while your mind listens. Allow your mind to reason while in tune with your heart. When your heart senses freedom, call forth a word, a picture, a description, or a story that captures the truth that enabled that feeling of freedom.

REFLECTION

REFLECTION

DAY 9 - SEPARATION

CONTEMPLATION

"Then God said, 'Let there be an expanse in the midst of the waters, and let it separate the waters from the waters.' God made the expanse, and separated the waters which were below the expanse from the waters which were above the expanse; and it was so. God called the expanse heaven. And there was evening and there was morning, a second day." (Genesis 1:6-8 NASB)

On day two, God voices an expanse to be in the midst of the waters. The expanse forms and causes a separation between the waters below the expanse from the waters above the expanse. The expanse is called heaven. This heaven is the earth's atmosphere. We live in this heaven!

In Spirit, we can also experience an inner heaven causing a separation within the soul. This heaven separates and makes a distinction between thoughts and feelings that are conditioned from our human nature, from thoughts and feelings that are conditioned from the Spirit.

In John 4, we learn about water that is from above. It is of the Spirit, called "living water." This "living water" is available to all who asks for it. It will become a well within everyone who asks, springing up unto eternal life.

PRACTICE

Read John 4:1-42.

No matter how we feel or who we have become, Jesus respects us as a human at any present time. It is important to be who we are while acknowledging our human nature. It is from her human nature, the Samaritan woman asked for living water. She was very open and honest with Jesus, even when it came to her private love affairs.

Find a comfortable quiet place.
Be still for at least three minutes. Focus on breathing.
Focus on being you (spirit).

Imagine coming to a well all alone with your water jug. As you approach the well, you see a man sitting next to it. You feel afraid. But, your thirst for water outweighs your fear. You meet Jesus and He shares with you about living water.

Acknowledge your human nature and current lifestyle.

Voice: "Lord, give me living water that only You can provide that will become in me a spring of water welling up to eternal life."
(repeat three times)

Allow your mind to give your heart freedom to feel.

Allow this time to continue for however long.

REFLECTION

Give yourself time to reflect through the day. If you choose, write or draw any reflections you experienced. Explore creativity, perhaps even recording your voice in words or song. This is to allow time for your heart and mind to have a conversation. Allow your heart to feel while your mind listens. Allow your mind to reason while in tune with your heart. When your heart senses freedom, call forth a word, a picture, a description, or a story that captures the truth that enabled that feeling of freedom.

REFLECTION

REFLECTION

DAY 10 - A SEED

CONTEMPLATION

"Then God said, 'Let the waters below the heavens be gathered into one place, and let the dry land appear'; and it was so. God called the dry land earth, and the gathering of the waters He called seas; and God saw that it was good. Then God said, 'Let the earth sprout vegetation, plants yielding seed, *and* fruit trees on the earth bearing fruit after their kind with seed in them'; and it was so. The earth brought forth vegetation, plants yielding seed after their kind, and trees bearing fruit with seed in them, after their kind; and God saw that it was good. There was evening and there was morning, a third day" (Genesis 1: 9-13 NASB).

Imagine the land emerging as it pushes up from under the waters. Can you hear the sounds of the waters rushing to one place as the land takes its place? Life then appears on the land in response to the vibration of the sound of God's voice. Not just one life, but life that reproduces life, with a seed.

A word or a phrase can be a seed of thought. A pat on the back or a hug can be a seed of feeling. A seed must penetrate the soul if it is to reproduce. A thought could have little affect if the heart is overwhelmed by loneliness. Likewise, a hug could have little affect if the mind is wrestling with thoughts. A seed can also come through watching. Watching others exchange forms of love can plant a seed of curiosity or desire, sparking the imagination.

Some seeds contain life, while others contain death. Both types of seed have the ability to penetrate the soul. All of us have these different types of seed growing within us. Some of us may feel more life, while others may feel more death.

No matter where we feel we are, through *in Spirit* living we learn to recognize good seed from bad seed. We recognize them from the fruit they produce.

As we begin to recognize the differences, practicing being *in Spirit* will allow God to plant and water good seed in our souls. God never plants or waters bad seed. The planting and watering of bad seed comes from our human nature, from our own or others. Practicing a harmful behavior waters a planted seed of a thought or a feeling containing death. This gives growth to the thought and feeling encouraging the behavior. It also can plant harmful seeds in others.

Bad seed can produce fruit that tastes good for a time and, at first, can even appear to be fruit of the Spirit. It is important to remember that the fruit of the Spirit is eternal and does not change over time. If we label a seed as good, and over time its fruit begins to tastes bad, it was never good or of the Spirit from the beginning. We misjudged.

God is the Master Sower of good seed. The planting and watering can come to us in many ways: from His Spirit, through thought or passion, from His word, through others, through creation, etc. Acknowledging these different ways will keep us from feeling codependent on anyone through whom God chooses to plant or water His good seed He has planted in our souls.

PRACTICE

Read Galatians 5:22-23. Paul describes the fruit of the Spirit to be: Love, Joy, Peace, Patience, Kindness, Goodness, Faithfulness, Gentleness, and Self-Control (spirit-control).

This means that by the mere life that is lived in fellowship with the Spirit will produce a life full of His fruit.

Find a comfortable quiet place.

Be still for at least three minutes. Focus on breathing.

Bring your thoughts to the fruit of the Spirit: Love.

How would you define this love?

Bring your emotions to the fruit of the Spirit: Love

How does this love make you feel?

Voice: "Father, may Your *love* flow from Your Spirit to my spirit into my heart and mind, flowing through my body"
(repeat three times)

Repeat this with each fruit of the Spirit: Joy, Peace, Patience, Kindness, Goodness, Faithfulness, Gentleness, Self-Control (spirit-control).

REFLECTION

Give yourself time to reflect through the day. If you choose, write or draw any reflections you experienced. Explore creativity, perhaps even recording your voice in words or song. This is to allow time for your heart and mind to have a conversation. Allow your heart to feel while your mind listens. Allow your mind to reason while in tune with your heart. When your heart senses freedom, call forth a word, a picture, a description, or a story that captures the truth that enabled that feeling of freedom.

REFLECTION

REFLECTION

DAY 11 - GOVERN

CONTEMPLATION

"And God said, 'Let there be lights in the expanse of the sky to separate the day from the night, and let them serve as signs to mark seasons and days and years, and let them be lights in the expanse of the sky to give light on the earth.' And it was so. God made two great lights—the greater light to govern the day and the lesser light to govern the night. He also made the stars. God set them in the expanse of the sky to give light on the earth, to govern the day and the night, and to separate light from darkness. And God saw that it was good. And there was evening, and there was morning—the fourth day" (Genesis 1:14-19 NIV).

On day four, God voices lights in the expanse of the heavens. This is another expanse (a heaven) separating heaven below (earth's atmosphere) from heaven above (a 3rd heaven). This heaven we call space. The purpose for these lights are: to serve as signs, to mark seasons, to designate days and years, and to give light on the earth. These lights are the sun, the moon, and the constellations of stars. The sun and moon give light on the earth, govern the day and the night, and separate light from darkness.

Being *in Spirit* allows Christ to shine light into our hearts and minds, to govern our hearts and minds, and separate light from darkness within our hearts and minds.

PRACTICE

"For God, who said, 'Let light shine out of darkness,' made His light shine in our hearts to give us the light of the knowledge of God's glory displayed in the face of Christ." (2 Corinthians 4:6 NIV)

Find a comfortable quiet place.

Be still for at least three minutes. Focus on breathing.

Voice: "Lord, I give You my heart and my mind, for Your light to shine on my soul to govern with kindness and gentleness."
(repeat three times)

Allow the mind to receive His light.

Voice: "I give You my mind to govern gently."
(repeat three times)

Allow the heart to receive His light.

Voice: "I give You my heart to condition with love."
(*repeat three times*)

Stay in this place of quiet for as long as you would like and feel free to fellowship however you may be led to participate.

REFLECTION

Give yourself time to reflect through the day. If you choose, write or draw any reflections you experienced. Explore creativity, perhaps even recording your voice in words or song. This is to allow time for your heart and mind to have a conversation. Allow your heart to feel while your mind listens. Allow your mind to reason while in tune with your heart. When your heart senses freedom, call forth a word, a picture, a description, or a story that captures the truth that enabled that feeling of freedom.

REFLECTION

REFLECTION

DAY 12 - MULTIPLY

CONTEMPLATION

"Then God said, 'Let the waters teem with swarms of living creatures, and let birds fly above the earth in the open expanse of the heavens.' God created the great sea monsters and every living creature that moves, with which the waters swarmed after their kind, and every winged bird after its kind; and God saw that it was good. God blessed them, saying, 'Be fruitful and multiply, and fill the waters in the seas, and let birds multiply on the earth.' There was evening and there was morning, a fifth day" (Genesis 1:20-23 NASB).

It is difficult to grasp the vastness of earth. We are blessed to have such technologies that allow us the opportunity to begin to understand the vastness of the ocean depths. The waters cover most of the earth's surface. Below the water's surface teems with life in a variety of shapes, sizes, and colors. Every detail has its place in the beauty of the whole.

Above the waters we have more opportunity to see the display of life in the heaven we live. Birds of various colors display their beautiful feathered bodies as they nest and fly. Every morning their songs can be heard.

When God creates life, He directs life to multiply. We experience this *in Spirit*. However we are by our human nature when we begin *in Spirit* is not how we will stay. Life-ways will replace death-ways, and will multiply.

113

As we continue *in Spirit*, our minds will teem with "Life Thoughts" and our hearts will teem with "Life Emotions." One thought will lead to another thought; one emotion will lead to another emotion. There is no end to this multiplication of life as long as we continue being *in Spirit*. For none of this renewing experience is being created by us. He who created everything outside us is creating everything new within us.

PRACTICE

As an ongoing practice: Take some time to learn about life in the oceans. Also, investigate the different types of birds in your area.

Having an aquarium and/or bird feeder, birdhouse, or hummingbird feeder invites natural sounds to a place of meditation. Watch birds to learn about them and to understand what Jesus says about them.

Imagine the mind being like the ocean and the heart being like the heaven.

Consider the fruit of the Spirit: Love, Joy, Peace, Patience, Kindness, Goodness, Faithfulness, Gentleness, and Self-Control (spirit-control).

PRACTICE

Find a comfortable quiet place.

Be still for at least three minutes. Focus on breathing.

Voice: "Lord, May Your voice echo through my mind and my heart to produce thoughts and emotions of life that will be fruitful and multiply."
(repeat three times)

Voice: "Lord, produce the fruit of *love* in my mind and heart and multiply *love* within my soul."
(repeat three times)

Voice the above replacing the word *love* with each fruit of the Spirit: Joy, Peace, Patience, Kindness, Gentleness, Faithfulness, Goodness, and Self-Control (spirit-control). Repeat each three times.

Stay in this place of quiet for as long as you would like.

Feel free to fellowship however you may be led to participate.

REFLECTION

Give yourself time to reflect through the day. If you choose, write or draw any reflections you experienced. Explore creativity, perhaps even recording your voice in words or song. This is to allow time for your heart and mind to have a conversation. Allow your heart to feel while your mind listens. Allow your mind to reason while in tune with your heart. When your heart senses freedom, call forth a word, a picture, a description, or a story that captures the truth that enabled that feeling of freedom.

REFLECTION

REFLECTION

DAY 13 - IN THE IMAGE OF GOD

CONTEMPLATION

"Then God said, 'Let the earth bring forth living creatures after their kind: cattle and creeping things and beasts of the earth after their kind'; and it was so. God made the beasts of the earth after their kind, and the cattle after their kind, and everything that creeps on the ground after its kind; and God saw that it was good. Then God said, 'Let Us make man in Our Image, according to Our likeness; and let them rule over the fish of the sea and over the birds of the sky and over the cattle and over all the earth, and over every creeping thing that creeps on the earth.' God created man in His own Image, in the Image of God He created him; male and female He created them. God blessed them; and God said to them, 'Be fruitful and multiply, and fill the earth, and subdue it; and rule over the fish of the sea and over the birds of the sky and over every living thing that moves on the earth.' Then God said, 'Behold, I have given you every plant yielding seed that is on the surface of all the earth, and every tree which has fruit yielding seed; it shall be food for you; and to every beast of the earth and to every bird of the sky and to every thing that moves on the earth which has life, *I have given* every green plant for food'; and it was so. God saw all that He had made, and behold, it was very good. And there was evening and there was morning, the sixth day." (Genesis 1: 24-31 NASB)

Read Genesis 2:4–3:7. Adam and Eve were created in the Image of God and according to His likeness. In comparison to everything else God created, it appears that man, though the last to be created, became first over everything created before him. We can conclude then that the greatest gift for any created being is to be a human. But it doesn't always feel this way, and we tend to have a hard time believing it. Why is this?

The description given in Genesis 1 is the way man was before he was led to disobey the commandment of God. It says that man was naked, and felt no shame (2:25), and later says that man's eyes were opened, and realized they were naked (3:7). They lost something that was keeping them from feeling shame, seeing their nakedness, and becoming mortal. Death entered into the human experience, through sin, which is not in God's Image. The immortal body experiencing love, through life in the Image of God, became a mortal body experiencing sin, through death in the image of mortal man.

Because our bodies are subject to death, we who are in Christ do not always feel we are in the Image of God. Occasionally, we wrestle with our awareness that we are immortal and are able to experience eternal love, through the life of Christ, who is the Image of God and in whom we dwell.

PRACTICE

Read Colossians 1:1–17.

Find a comfortable quiet.

Be still for at least three minutes. Focus on breathing.

Allow your thoughts to imagine being clothed with a body of light that covers your nakedness.

All you see is light. This is God's Image. This is Christ.

Allow the light of Christ to enlighten the heart to feel, and the mind to flow with thought.

Voice: "The light of Christ covers everything, for in Him all things were created. This includes me."
(repeat three times)

Throughout your day:

Reflect on any passion that arises within the heart or thought that enters in the mind. Take note of any other ways God is speaking (through His word, through creation, through others) that confirm the passion or thought?

REFLECTION

Give yourself time to reflect through the day. If you choose, write or draw any reflections you experienced. Explore creativity, perhaps even recording your voice in words or song. This is to allow time for your heart and mind to have a conversation. Allow your heart to feel while your mind listens. Allow your mind to reason while in tune with your heart. When your heart senses freedom, call forth a word, a picture, a description, or a story that captures the truth that enabled that feeling of freedom.

REFLECTION

DAY 14 - REST

CONTEMPLATION

"Thus the heavens and the earth were completed, and all their hosts. By the seventh day God completed His work which He had done, and He rested on the seventh day from all His work which He had done. Then God blessed the seventh day and sanctified it, because in it He rested from all His work which God had created and made" (Genesis 2:1-3 NASB).

The way God creates demonstrates His divine nature and eternal power. To know His divine nature and eternal power enables us to participate in them. In the way the creation account is written shows us:

Day 1:	Darkness before Light
Day 2:	Water below before Water above
Day 3:	Land below water before Land above
Day 4:	Evening before Morning, therefore Lesser light (moon) before Greater light (sun)
Day 5:	Fish (descending creatures), before Birds (Ascending creatures)
Day 6:	Animals (to be ruled) before Man (to rule)

Through what is made we can clearly see that descending comes before ascending. God's divine nature is to descend to serve, and His eternal power is to raise up (ascend or resurrect). It clearly portrays the lesser before the greater. What is last will be first and what is first will be last.

God's invisible qualities (His divine nature and eternal power) are opposite our often, visible qualities, brought about by our human sinful nature. The human sinful nature is to descend others to serve self and to ascend self to feel power or above others. Pride is often what we feel and show when we allow the human sinful nature to govern the mind and heart. Struggles with other sins follow hiding the root of all sins, pride. We struggle with sin when we desire to be a superhero (a god) seeking the praise or applause of men, to win, to have dominion over everything, to be something, to be great, to leave behind a legacy, to rule, to have a family name that lasts forever . . . the list can go on and on.

When the human sinful nature governs the mind and heart, it causes a lot of work and stress attempting to stay ahead as we compare ourselves to others or a better version of ourselves. *In Spirit*, we discover rest allowing the Spirit to govern the mind and heart giving a new perspective. As we transition between these two perspectives, we will find ourselves more inclined to our gifts and how to use those gifts to help others.

PRACTICE

Make a list of ways you have put yourself before others.

Or, be watchful for the times when you put yourself before others, then:

Consider the motivation for each time.

In what way would you have acted differently and why?

PRACTICE

Read 2 Peter 1:3-8.

Find a comfortable quiet place to be still.

Be still for at least three minutes. Focus on breathing.

Voice: "May I participate in Your divine nature as Your nature lives through me by Your Spirit. May I grow to know all Your great and precious promises as I grow to know the glory and goodness of Jesus Christ."
(repeat three times)

Consider what Peter shares for growth: faith, goodness, knowledge, self-control, perseverance, godliness, mutual affection, and love.

Throughout the day:

Give the Spirit access to govern the mind and heart.

Allow the Spirit to guide you through faith, goodness, knowledge, self-control, perseverance, godliness, mutual affection, and love.

Be open to change.

REFLECTION

Give yourself time to reflect through the day. If you choose, write or draw any reflections you experienced. Explore creativity, perhaps even recording your voice in words or song. This is to allow time for your heart and mind to have a conversation. Allow your heart to feel while your mind listens. Allow your mind to reason while in tune with your heart. When your heart senses freedom, call forth a word, a picture, a description, or a story that captures the truth that enabled that feeling of freedom.

REFLECTION

REFLECTION

DAYS 15 THROUGH 21

JESUS AS HUMAN
ATTITUDE
FAITH
HOPE
LOVE
LAW AND SIN
GRACE AND TRUTH

BEFORE YOU BEGIN DAY 15...

During these next seven days, I will guide you through a special journey as we gaze deeper into the life of Christ. We will listen to Jesus' words concerning Himself in order to better understand how He was capable of pouring forth such great love in every situation, especially the difficult ones. If we come to know His faith, then we can begin to participate in His truth, and experience His life with our own.

Jesus' model of aligning Himself with the Father provides a starting point. Intentional *in Spirit* living is vital to harmonize our attitudes, in the faith, hope, and love of Christ. The heart and mind will grow in renewed desire, passion, thought, eagerness, and will.

Once we have a glimpse of Jesus' exemplary life, we will explore law and sin, followed by grace and truth. There is a difference between these two ways in which one can live. Understanding how a mind governed by a set of rules can keep one bound to repetitive, negative behavioral patterns is important to deter away from that way of life. We can begin to turn toward a new way of living where the Spirit governs the mind. This new way is a liberating and the experience will allow the fruit of the Spirit to resonate within the soul, bringing healing to the heart and mind.

Again, give time for your mind and heart to grow together. **Set a pace that works best for you.**

DAY 15 - JESUS AS HUMAN

CONTEMPLATION

When we consider Jesus, we notice something so profound from that of ourselves—a human nature in which the Spirit of God governs the mind and heart. Humility is what Jesus felt and demonstrated. Humility allowed Jesus to stand up under temptation, never experiencing sin (which is defined as a mastering of the soul to go against God's way, truth, and life).

In John 14, Jesus shares with His disciples exactly how He was living on earth in a human body. He reveals to them His spiritual makeup and continues to reveal to them the spiritual makeup of whoever chooses to live by faith.

In John 14, after Philip asks Jesus to show them the Father (God), Jesus explains to the disciples that the Father was living in Him. Jesus further stated it this way, "I am in the Father and the Father is in me." (The group of circles in the practice section illustrates this *in Spirit* experience. Color the circles as instructed.)

Verse 12 is very profound. Jesus says that anyone who has faith in Him will not only do what He had been doing, but will do even greater things than these, because Jesus was going to the Father. When Jesus returned to the Father, He was able to fill the entire universe as Spirit (Ephesians 4:10). The only difference between the spiritual makeup of Jesus and one who has faith in Jesus is Jesus Himself. While on earth He is human; in us, He is Spirit.

Verse 10, Jesus says that it is the Father doing the work that they have been witnessing through the body of Jesus. The reason we are able to experience greater things than what Jesus did is because of Jesus living in us *in Spirit*. Father and Son, and Holy Spirit can work through us, just as the Father and Holy Spirit worked through Jesus. In fact, Jesus says if we ask anything in His Name that He would do it. He is capable of doing it through us because He lives within us. It is time for us to surrender. It is time to ask for Him to do what was planned for Him to do within us and through us since before the creation of the world.

PRACTICE

JESUS AS HUMAN

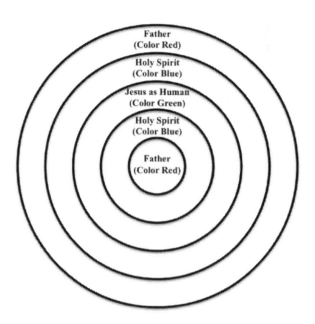

PRACTICE

YOU WHO LIVE BY FAITH

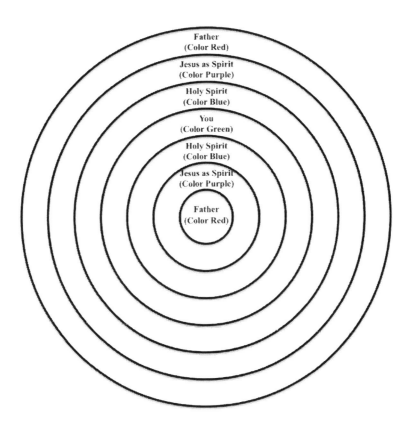

PRACTICE

Read John 14.

Find a comfortable, quiet place.

Acknowledge that the Father, Jesus, and Holy Spirit can live through you.

Turn your attention to the circles representing you in God and God in you (you who live by faith). If you have not already done so, color the circles as indicated.

Be still for at least three minutes. Focus on breathing.

Imagine being a green sphere of light.

Three other light spheres approach you. They are different in color.

Blue light falls upon you and fills you. This is Holy Spirit. You feel comfort, support, and that you are heard.

Purple light falls upon you and fills you. This is Jesus as Spirit. You feel a common likeness, an understanding, and a sense of peace.

Red light falls upon you and fills you. This is the Father. You feel eternal love and grace. You feel rooted and established. You feel power and experience within you: Love, Joy, Peace, Patience, Kindness, Goodness, Faithfulness, Gentleness, and Self-Control (spirit-control).

PRACTICE

Voice: "Father, Jesus, Holy Spirit. Come live in me and live through me. Grant to me the grace and the peace that will allow me to rest in You. I live in You, and You live in me." *(repeat three times)*

Walking in life the way Jesus did encompasses total surrender to the Father, Jesus, and Holy Spirit in every aspect of life.

Throughout the day:

Be mindful that God desires to live through your body.

Be watchful of ways He lives through you.

REFLECTION

Give yourself time to reflect through the day. If you choose, write or draw any reflections you experienced. Explore creativity, perhaps even recording your voice in words or song. This is to allow time for your heart and mind to have a conversation. Allow your heart to feel while your mind listens. Allow your mind to reason while in tune with your heart. When your heart senses freedom, call forth a word, a picture, a description, or a story that captures the truth that enabled that feeling of freedom.

REFLECTION

REFLECTION

DAY 16 - ATTITUDE

CONTEMPLATION

"Do nothing from selfishness or empty conceit, but with humility of mind regard one another as more important than yourselves; do not *merely* look out for your own personal interests, but also for the interests of others. Have this attitude in yourselves, which was also in Christ Jesus, who, although He existed in the form of God, did not regard equality with God a thing to be grasped, but emptied Himself, taking the form of a bond-servant, *and* being made in the likeness of men. Being found in appearance as a man, He humbled Himself by becoming obedient to the point of death, even death on a cross. For this reason also, God highly exalted Him, and bestowed on Him the Name which is above every name, so that at the Name of Jesus every knee will bow, of those who are in heaven and on earth and under the earth, and that every tongue will confess that Jesus Christ is Lord, to the glory of God the Father." (Philippians 2:3-11 NASB)

Though we may believe in Jesus, have knowledge of scripture, and even have scripture memorized, if Jesus' attitude is not firmly within our character, then the opportunity to experience God's power in our lives will be lost. An attitude adjustment is crucial to transform us to experience the likeness of Christ.

We do not necessarily have to force an attitude of humility, but simply experience the flow of humility from Christ (who lives in us) as we are *in Spirit*. When we are in tuned to everything within us and everything outside ourselves is in Christ, His greatness causes our knee to bow and our tongue to voice, "Jesus Christ is Lord."

While on earth, Jesus understood the greatness of His heavenly Father. As a result, He chose to empty Himself, recognizing His humanness, setting His mind toward serving. This way of practice kept pride from developing in His soul and allowed the Father the use of His body to live in and through. With this same attitude, Father, Jesus, and the Holy Spirit can live through us today.

My attitude wavers. To remain humble is a difficult challenge for me when things do not go my way. Often times I allow pride to govern my actions and words. Being *in Spirit* gives me this awareness of self, helps me understand that God's love for me is unwavering, and humbles me in the process giving me the assurance that... I'm OKAY! We are never without need of the blood of Jesus.

PRACTICE

Read John 13: 1-17.

Find a comfortable, quiet place.

Be still for at least three minutes. Focus on breathing.

Acknowledge that the Father, Jesus, and the Holy Spirit are living in you.

Surrender to them to take control and to live in and through you.

Voice: "Jesus is Lord."
(*repeat three times*)

Voice: "I descend myself so that You, Father, may ascend Yourself, Jesus, Holy Spirit, and me together as one into a new experiential life, You in me and I in You."
(*repeat three times*)

PRACTICE

Feel God's power through humility.

Is there someone in your life whom you love but you feel is less fortunate?

What are their needs? Which one do you feel is the greatest need?

Give this to Christ living in you. If and when you are moved by compassion, allow Christ to move through you to serve.

Voice: "Father, I open my heart and mind to You. Guide me to listen. Move me with compassion. Allow me to experience your Spirit move through my body to serve." (*repeat three times*)

REFLECTION

Give yourself time to reflect through the day. If you choose, write or draw any reflections you experienced. Explore creativity, perhaps even recording your voice in words or song. This is to allow time for your heart and mind to have a conversation. Allow your heart to feel while your mind listens. Allow your mind to reason while in tune with your heart. When your heart senses freedom, call forth a word, a picture, a description, or a story that captures the truth that enabled that feeling of freedom.

REFLECTION

REFLECTION

DAY 17 - FAITH

CONTEMPLATION

Faith is a word we commonly use. What does it mean to have faith? There are many promises to those who have faith in Jesus, so it is important to understand faith.

In Romans 4, Paul explains faith by describing the faith of Abraham. Let's take a look at how faith is defined in the faith of Abraham.

Verse 5:   Abraham believed and trusted in a God who forgives sins (justifies the ungodly).

Verse 17:   Abraham believed in a God that gives life to the dead (resurrection).
Abraham believed in a God that calls into being things that were not.

Verse 21:   Abraham believed in a God that had power to do what He had promised.

If we are to have the faith of Abraham, we must believe God forgives sins, raises the dead, creates things out of nothing, and has power to do what He has promised. God does all of this through Jesus Christ. Faith in Jesus sums up the faith of Abraham. As God credited Abraham with righteousness, God credits righteousness to anyone who has faith in Jesus. God is able to credit righteousness because God forgives sins, raises the dead, creates things out of nothing, and fulfills His promises through Jesus Christ.

Faith is a gift from God given to all men. However, it is our will that chooses where we place His gift of faith. We sometimes place faith in ourselves, other people, animals, things, churches, jobs, talents, money, etc. We eventually realize we can become easily disappointed in all these things. These things do not fulfill our soul's need for comfort that lasts, the fruit of the Spirit.

Faith in Jesus must penetrate the soul and body. Faith will cause our minds to believe in, our hearts to confess of, and our bodies to express the death, burial, and resurrection of Jesus Christ by submitting to the command to be immersed in water. Faith in Jesus unites our souls and bodies to Him (see Romans 6). Faith penetrates all parts of being human so that everything can be fully His.

PRACTICE

Read Romans 4 – 6.

Find a comfortable, quiet place.

Be still for at least three minutes. Focus on breathing.

Voice: "I believe that You, Jesus, are the Christ, the Son of the Living God, through whom the Father chooses to forgive sins, to give life to the dead, to create things out of nothing, and to keep all His promises to us." *(repeat three times)*

Allow this belief to flow through the mind.

Allow this confession to flow through the heart.

Give Jesus your body, remembering your baptism.

PRACTICE

Acknowledge that the Father, Jesus, and Holy Spirit are living in you and are all around you.

Surrender yourself to your Father, your Lord, and your Comforter to take control to live in and through you.

Voice: "I give You my spirit, my heart, my mind, and my body to accomplish Your will in me and through me. Not my will, but Your will be done in me and through me, in Jesus' Name, AMEN."
(repeat three times)

REFLECTION

Give yourself time to reflect through the day. If you choose write or draw any reflections you experienced. Explore creativity, perhaps even recording your voice in words or song. This is to allow time for your heart and mind to have a conversation. Allow your heart to feel while your mind listens. Allow your mind to reason while in tune with your heart. When your heart senses freedom, call forth a word, a picture, a description, or a story that captures the truth that enabled that feeling of freedom.

REFLECTION

REFLECTION

DAY 18 - HOPE

CONTEMPLATION

Having faith in Jesus gives us hope that is not conditioned by what we can see. Abraham and his wife, Sarah, were well over the years of child bearing. But by faith, Abraham believed God at His word and had hope that they indeed would have a son, even though, naturally, it seemed unbelievable.

"Therefore, since we have been justified through faith, we have peace with God through our Lord Jesus Christ, through whom we have gained access by faith into this grace in which we now stand. And we boast in the hope of the glory of God. Not only so, but we also glory in our sufferings, because we know that suffering produces perseverance; perseverance, character; and character, hope. And hope does not put us to shame, because God's love has been poured out into our hearts through the Holy Spirit, who has been given to us." (Romans 5: 1-5 NIV)

Through faith in Jesus, we gain access to grace and peace, through which we can hope that God's glory will be revealed in us. This hope gives us the ability to glory in our sufferings we feel from the body, through the soul.

To feel hope, we must first experience a suffering to produce perseverance, to produce Godly character, to produce this hope. This ever-increasing experience will awaken us even more to God's love and how He does live in us through His Spirit. This is an experience of immortality *in Spirit* while experiencing mortality in the body.

This hope with God's love in our hearts through His Spirit takes away our shame. With Abraham and Sarah, it was the shame of not having a son. With us, it is any shame we may feel as a result of being mortal. With hope, we know our bodies one day will be transformed and also experience immortality. This also is the glory of God.

PRACTICE

Select an action or a behavior you keep doing that is harmful to you (emotionally, mentally, and/or physically) and/or others that you desire to stop but find it difficult.

Find a quiet, comfortable place.

Be still for at least three minutes. Focus on breathing.

Voice: "Father, I give You my body as a living sacrifice, holy and blameless. Not because of anything I have done but because of everything You have done through the body and blood of Jesus. I give You my mind to govern with Your thoughts and I give You my heart to condition with your love. Come live in me and live through me. Bestow Your Spirit upon me and fill me within with Your very presence. May I feel the fruit of Your Spirit: Love, Joy, Peace, Patience, Kindness, Gentleness, Faithfulness, Goodness, and Self-Control. In Jesus Name, AMEN."
(*repeat three times*)

Continue this fellowship for as long as you desire.

Throughout the day, walk in mindfulness, remembering that you are spirit and that God lives in you. Also, keep your attention on what things God does through you. Journal the experiences, noting any new thoughts and any acts of love.

PRACTICE

Temptation will come to act out the behavior of which you are trying to quit. When you feel the temptation approaching, acknowledge the pursuit of comfort.

Voice: "Lord Jesus, come fill me with the comfort that I am seeking that only You can provide: The eternal comfort of Love, Joy, Peace, Patience, Kindness, Gentleness, Faithfulness, Goodness, Self-Control. In Your Name I pray, AMEN."

There will be a suffering felt within you by not allowing temptation to perform through the body. The body will feel this suffering. During this suffering, call upon the Name of the Lord, using the prayer above as a template. Also, try comforting the body through healthy means such as a shower or a bath, or go for a walk.

The temptation will subside eventually, and you will reap a reward of Joy. The mind and heart will feel a sense of unity. This experience will awaken perseverance. During the next season of temptation, remembering the joy, unity and freedom you had after overcoming your recent trial will give reason to persevere once again.

Make this a daily practice, and over time, a new character (or *charism*) will emerge. This will increase faith and hope and awaken you to God's love and power through His Holy Spirit, which is made possible through Jesus Christ.

REFLECTION

Give yourself time to reflect through the day. If you choose, write or draw any reflections you experienced. Explore creativity, perhaps even recording your voice in words or song. This is to allow time for your heart and mind to have a conversation. Allow your heart to feel while your mind listens. Allow your mind to reason while in tune with your heart. When your heart senses freedom, call forth a word, a picture, a description, or a story that captures the truth that enabled that feeling of freedom.

REFLECTION

REFLECTION

DAY 19 - LOVE

CONTEMPLATION

"You see, at just the right time, when we were still powerless, Christ died for the ungodly. Very rarely will anyone die for a righteous person, though for a good person someone might possibly dare to die. But God demonstrates his own love for us in this: While we were still sinners, Christ died for us.
Since we have now been justified by His blood, how much more shall we be saved from God's wrath through Him! For if, while we were God's enemies, we were reconciled to Him through the death of His Son, how much more, having been reconciled, shall we be saved through His life! Not only is this so, but we also boast in God through our Lord Jesus Christ, through whom we have now received reconciliation." (Romans 5: 6-11 NIV)

Wow! What an amazing love we are shown by God, through Jesus Christ. This love is contagious, and once felt, the soul of man rises to shine through His life. It is through the blood of Christ that our sins are atoned and allows us the opportunity to have faith that God does forgive sins. Therefore, we can forgive ourselves, and forgive anyone who has sinned against us. God is love!

Forgiving someone does not come so easy for me, especially when I feel justice needs to be served. I feel if I forgive them, justice won't be served. They need to feel my pain, so I convince myself to keep holding a grudge. This affects my ability to live abundantly.

PRACTICE

Make a list of people you feel you have wronged or have wronged you in the past. Will you extend an apology or allow yourself to forgive them?

When we feel someone has hurt us, we may feel resentment toward that person. The resentment is felt as a result of being treated as less than equal. Our reaction compensates the feeling of less than and we push back. Unaware we have placed that person below ourselves, elevating us above that one. Unknowingly, pride has secretly made its way into our hearts.

When we forgive, we are on equal levels, and pride is extinguished. Forgiving does not make us less than.

If you are finding it difficult to forgive, what is keeping you from doing so? Is it the pain you feel? Is it pride?

Pride is the root of all sin. If we do not extinguish our pride, then our quality of life will not be the best it could be.

By Jesus saying, "Father, forgive them, for they don't know what they are doing" (Luke 23:34, NLT), gave no room for pride to set up in His heart keeping Him innocent of sin.

When people wrong us, we feel some form of justice should be served. Justice has been served when we accept the spilt blood of Christ to be not only for us, but also for those who sin against us.

PRACTICE

Jesus could forgive sins because the justice requirement for killing an innocent man was applied on the innocent man Himself.

Applying the blood of Jesus is the first step toward forgiving unconditionally and loving even an enemy. *In Spirit* living provides the blood (sacrifice) and power to forgive any enemy.

Find a comfortable, quiet place.
Be still for at least three minutes. Focus on breathing.

Voice: "Through Your blood and Spirit You love me and forgive me. Through Your blood and Spirit I now love and forgive (say a name of one on the list). Bless them by Your presence so that they too may one day experience Your love. Bless me with the understanding of Your truth that I belong and I am enough. You in me and I in You."
(*repeat this for all on the list*)

If you are having trouble forgiving, ask the Lord to show you what is keeping you from an apology or the ability to forgive.

The Spirit of the Lord is very patient and does not leave you if you are finding it difficult to forgive someone.

Continue to move through your heart and mind until you are able to forgive. Forgiveness is important to the healing of the soul and experiencing abundant life.

REFLECTION

Give yourself time to reflect through the day. If you choose, write or draw any reflections you experienced. Explore creativity, perhaps even recording your voice in words or song. This is to allow time for your heart and mind to have a conversation. Allow your heart to feel while your mind listens. Allow your mind to reason while in tune with your heart. When your heart senses freedom, call forth a word, a picture, a description, or a story that captures the truth that enabled that feeling of freedom.

REFLECTION

DAY 20 - LAW AND SIN

CONTEMPLATION

Have you ever felt guilt? What made you feel guilty? Guilt is felt when one violates the law of one's own mind. If you are in a habitual cycle of an activity that you desire to stop, and you set your mind on not doing that activity, chances are you will find it extremely difficult to be faithful to that law you placed before yourself. In addition, you may live with guilt and in shame. This affects one's mood and one's relationships.

Why is it difficult to overcome addiction? Paul shares in Romans 7 that sin is living and dwelling within us, producing desires and thoughts. Law, when applied, gives sin an opportunity to manifest its desires and thoughts to overpower our own minds and hearts.

Paul gives a personal example of his ways of coveting. If he tries to not covet with the mind, he covets. If he tries to not covet with the heart, he covets. Paul concludes that there is nothing in himself that can keep him from coveting. When he attempts to refrain, sin wins, and he commits sin. However, when he does sin, with his soul in resistance to sin, he concludes that it is not him, but sin living him that is doing it.

Sin is more than just the bad things we do and feel are contrary to what God would have us do. Sin is a living entity having access to our thoughts and emotions.

Analytically studying the Bible, seeking to prove a behavior right or wrong, is seeking a law in an attempt to feel comfort on "right" behavior. When we do this, sin will seize this opportunity afforded by the law to continue to subject its will over our soul (mind and heart).

Eventually we will come to a conclusion, as Paul did, that we live in a body that is subject to death. But the good news is that law is not all we have. We have grace given to us from God, through Jesus Christ.

PRACTICE

Read Romans 7.

Make a list describing the purpose of law?

What kind of man does Paul declare himself to be attempting to live holy by law?

What does it feel like to be wretched?

Have you ever feel wretched?

PRACTICE

Find a comfortable, quiet place.

Be still for at least three minutes. Focus on breathing.

Acknowledge that the Father, Jesus, and the Holy Spirit are living in you.

Allow the light of Christ to expose any areas of the soul where the mind judges the heart.

Allow the light of Christ to expose any areas of the soul where the heart hates the mind.

Allow the light of Christ to allow the mind to forgive the heart and the heart to love the mind.

Voice: "Father, thank You for providing a more freeing way to live through Your Son, Jesus Christ. Through His blood and His Spirit, I can live by grace and truth." *(repeat three times)*

REFLECTION

Give yourself time to reflect through the day. If you choose, write or draw any reflections you experienced. Explore creativity, perhaps even recording your voice in words or song. This is to allow time for your heart and mind to have a conversation. Allow your heart to feel while your mind listens. Allow your mind to reason while in tune with your heart. When your heart senses freedom, call forth a word, a picture, a description, or a story that captures the truth that enabled that feeling of freedom.

REFLECTION

REFLECTION

DAY 21 - GRACE AND TRUTH

CONTEMPLATION

"For the Law was given through Moses; grace and truth were realized through Jesus Christ." (John 1:17 NASB)

After tasting the fruit from the tree of knowledge of good and evil, Adam and Eve felt shame because they became fully aware of good and evil. As their offspring, we, by nature, know good and evil. When we participate in evil, we feel guilt and, sometimes, shame. When we practice good, we feel better. Many religions are based on this concept and have created laws or doctrines to distinguish between good and evil. These influence our minds. As a result, a law of our mind is at work defending and accusing our desires, thoughts and actions.

When God chose Abraham, it was because of his faith. To Abraham's natural descendants, through Isaac and Jacob, God instituted a religion based on the Law given to them through Moses. Its purpose was to show man that religion based on the knowledge of good and evil only exposes sin living within us. Sin without the law remains unseen. When the Law appeared sin within began to use the Law to produce experiences of death. Though the Law of Moses is holy, righteous and just, its only purpose is to guide us to understanding sin and prompt us to search for a more freeing way of living.

In Christ, we have died as a child of the old Adam and have become a child of a new Adam, who has tasted the fruit from the tree of life. His offspring have a spiritual desire to experience life. The life of Christ provides grace and truth and gives power through that grace to inherit the kingdom of God, a way to stand up under temptation, reigning with Christ within one's own heart. This can only be accomplished through His Spirit, not through any law.

The Lord knows our hearts and He understands this more than we do. That is why Christ died, so that we might have the opportunity to live in a way, though we experience sin's thoughts and passions, to experience the power of God's Spirit conquering the sin living in us, through *in Spirit* living.

PRACTICE

Read Romans 5:12-21.

Make a list comparing Adam to Jesus.

Make a list comparing an offspring of Adam to an offspring of Jesus.

How are many made righteous?

What must reign to bring eternal life through Jesus Christ?

Find a comfortable, quiet place.

Be still for at least three minutes. Focus on breathing.

Acknowledge that the Father, Jesus, and the Holy Spirit live in you.

PRACTICE

Realize the grace and truth available through Jesus Christ.

Allow grace and truth to begin their reign in you.

Feel grace flow within your spirit.

Feel truth flow within your spirit.

Allow the flow of grace and truth into your heart.

Allow the flow of grace and truth into your mind.

Give your body to grace and truth to reign through you.

Voice: "Lord, may grace and truth that You bring reign throughout my entirety. I give You my spirit, my heart, my mind, and my body to cultivate with Your Spirit of grace and truth."
(repeat three times)

REFLECTION

Give yourself time to reflect through the day. If you choose, write or draw any reflections you experienced. Explore creativity, perhaps even recording your voice in words or song. This is to allow time for your heart and mind to have a conversation. Allow your heart to feel while your mind listens. Allow your mind to reason while in tune with your heart. When your heart senses freedom, call forth a word, a picture, a description, or a story that captures the truth that enabled that feeling of freedom.

REFLECTION

REFLECTION

DAYS 22 THROUGH 28

LIFE ACCORDING TO THE SPIRIT
THE IMAGE OF GOD
LIVING SACRIFICE
CONSCIENCE
SUBCONSCIOUS
BODY AND SOUL CYCLES
THE INNER GARDEN

BEFORE YOU BEGIN DAY 22...

We began with the basics of being human, growing in an awareness of what it means to have a spirit, heart, mind and body. We looked at creation as a way to understand how a new creation could take place within us. We then carefully listened to Jesus as He disclosed how He was living giving attention to attitude, faith, hope, and love. We have compared the power of law with grace and truth. Grace and truth given through Jesus Christ empowers us to experience an abundant life, which by any law we cannot obtain.

These next seven days plunge us into a deeper awareness unveiling aspects of ourselves. We start at discussing life according to the Spirit. We then focus on Jesus being the Image of God and how we fit in that Image. We begin to accept the fact that offering our bodies as living sacrifices is a crucial step to this new life.

Next, we bring to the attention the conscience, subconscious, and body and soul cycles. These will reveal challenges we will face as we pursue a renewed life. Lastly, we give a strategy of staying within the inner garden and working out from the inner garden of the heart.

DAY 22 - LIFE ACCORDING TO THE SPIRIT

CONTEMPLATION

Being *in Spirit* allows the soul (mind and heart) to be governed by the indwelling Spirit of Holy Spirit, Christ, and Father. When we allow Them to govern, we experience life according to the Spirit.

Just as national laws govern us and those that violate those laws are brought to justice, the knowledge of good and evil governs our human nature. Sin draws strength from this knowledge overpowering the soul. When we participate in sin, the righteous justice requirement is death.

As we experience life according to the Spirit, we feel no condemnation, because the righteous requirement of the law has been met through the death of Jesus. This sets us free from the knowledge of good and evil. We are born again in God's Image. Jesus Christ, and it is He who governs our souls. Life according to the Spirit will prompt our hearts and set our minds on new desires and passions, and will set our minds. Our souls will feel free, full of life and peace.

The body, however, is still subject to physical death. It will continue to grow old and can experience pain, sickness, and disease. But because the Spirit of God lives in us, the Father, who raised Jesus from the dead, will also raise us up, granting life to our mortal bodies, transforming and making them immortal.

Life according to the Spirit grants us to be children of God, brings about our adoption to sonship, and gives us the right to call God our "Abba" (daddy), Father. Being *in Spirit* will testify that we are God's children. By being a child of God, we are heirs of God and co-heirs with Christ. We experience hope through the sufferings we feel as we transition from our old way to the new way of living. The experiential glory surpasses the momentary sufferings we encounter.

All of creation is waiting for a resurrection. Experiencing life according to the Spirit through *in Spirit* living connects us to all of creation. As our bodies wait in eagerness for life, we can sympathize with everything that may feel pain. So we care and love all created things, especially other humans.

The Holy Spirit is our comforter, helper, and intercessor. He prays for us with groans that cannot be expressed through words. In addition, the Father works for the good of those who love Him.

PRACTICE

Read Romans 8.

Make a list of promises that come through the life according to the Spirit.

Find a comfortable, quiet place.

Be still for at least three minutes. Focus on breathing.

Acknowledge that the Father, Jesus, and Holy Spirit are living in you.

With faith, claim ownership of God's promises.

Voice: "Father, through the blood and Spirit of Jesus Christ there is now no condemnation for me. May this truth grow within my soul enabling me to feel this freedom and to keep my mind governed by the Spirit so I can experience life and peace."
(repeat three times)

REFLECTION

Give yourself time to reflect through the day. If you choose, write or draw any reflections you experienced. Explore creativity, perhaps even recording your voice in words or song. This is to allow time for your heart and mind to have a conversation. Allow your heart to feel while your mind listens. Allow your mind to reason while in tune with your heart. When your heart senses freedom, call forth a word, a picture, a description, or a story that captures the truth that enabled that feeling of freedom.

REFLECTION

DAY 23 - THE IMAGE OF GOD

CONTEMPLATION

Living according to the Spirit means God lives in us and we live in Him. As we engage this relationship through *In Spirit* living, we begin to walk out our earthly lives just as Jesus walked.

Living this new way will attract people to you, just as people were attracted to Jesus. It is important to remain humble. The attitude of humility is a very important component to living according to the Spirit. It is the Image of God penetrating the world through you while you remain in His Image.

There will be others who are jealous of your way of attraction. Jesus faced this reaction from the religious leaders of His time. It is important, still, to remain humble and to understand where that jealousy is coming from within the individual.

"The Son is the Image of the invisible God, the firstborn over all creation. For in Him all things were created: things in heaven and on earth, visible and invisible, whether thrones or powers or rulers or authorities; all things have been created through Him and for Him. He is before all things, and in Him all things hold together. And He is the head of the body, the church; He is the beginning and the firstborn from among the dead, so that in everything He might have the supremacy. For God was pleased to have all His fullness dwell in Him, and through Him to reconcile to Himself all things, whether things on earth or things in heaven, by making peace through His blood, shed on the cross." (Colossians 1:15-20 NIV)

Living according to the Spirit is just an opportunity to participate in the work the Image of God chooses to do through you. You will encounter very special and unique opportunities that will aid in you coming to know Him. Other opportunities will be with others living according to the Spirit. It is important to be mindful that all things were created in Him, through Him, and for Him. This will open the eyes of your heart to receive Him through all things.

PRACTICE

Find a comfortable, quiet place.

Be still for at least three minutes. Focus on breathing.

Voice: "Lord Jesus, You are the Image of God. Thank You for Your love for me that enables me to participate in You. Open my eyes to see You, my ears to hear You, and my hands to feel You through all things. Penetrate my heart and my mind. Move me with love and compassion through renewed thoughts and passions." (*repeat three times*)

Walk in mindfulness throughout the day, acknowledging Christ lives in you.

Be attentive to ways in which the Lord may be guiding you.

Are there any common themes you notice through conversation, imagery, songs, or from other sources?

REFLECTION

Give yourself time to reflect through the day. If you choose, write or draw any reflections you experienced. Explore creativity, perhaps even recording your voice in words or song. This is to allow time for your heart and mind to have a conversation. Allow your heart to feel while your mind listens. Allow your mind to reason while in tune with your heart. When your heart senses freedom, call forth a word, a picture, a description, or a story that captures the truth that enabled that feeling of freedom.

REFLECTION

DAY 24 - LIVING SACRIFICE

CONTEMPLATION

"And so, dear brothers and sisters, I plead with you to give your bodies to God because of all He has done for you. Let them be a living and holy sacrifice—the kind He will find acceptable. This is truly the way to worship Him. Don't copy the behavior and customs of this world, but let God transform you into a new person by changing the way you think. Then you will learn to know God's will for you, which is good and pleasing and perfect." (Romans 12:1-2 NLT)

Giving our bodies as a means for God to penetrate the world is very important. We are spirit, and we live in our bodies. How connected are we to our bodies? We can see with our eyes, we can hear with our ears, we can serve with our hands, we can feel with our hearts, and we can think with our minds. God is also Spirit and lives in us, so can He not, then, choose to see with our eyes, hear with our ears, serve with our hands, feel with our hearts, and even think with our minds?

If we daily give our bodies to Him to live in and live through, we will experience a shift in the way we think. We will learn how to listen to Him and be guided in this life into a good and pleasing and perfect will He has planned for us.

PRACTICE

Find a comfortable, quiet place.

Be still for at least three minutes. Focus on breathing.

Voice:
"Our Father, who dwells in heaven, hallowed be Your Name. Your reign come. Your will be done.
In our spirits as it is in Your Spirit.
In our hearts as it is in Your heart.
In our minds as it is in Your mind.
Give us this day our daily spiritual food.
Allow us to experience the way You shepherd us out of temptation.
Allow us to experience the way You deliver us from evil.
For to You belong the eternal kingdom, with all glory and all power, forever and ever.
We give You our bodies as living sacrifices, holy and pleasing. Not because of anything we have done, but because of everything You have done through Jesus Christ. Come live in us, and live through us.
Fill us with Your Holy Spirit.
May we feel the fruit of Your Spirit: Love, Joy, Peace, Patience, Kindness, Goodness, Faithfulness, Gentleness and Self Control.
Allow this to be our source of comfort.
In Jesus Name, AMEN."

Walk in mindfulness throughout the day, acknowledging Christ lives in you. Be attentive to ways in which the Lord may be guiding you.

REFLECTION

Give yourself time to reflect through the day. If you choose, write or draw any reflections you experienced. Explore creativity, perhaps even recording your voice in words or song. This is to allow time for your heart and mind to have a conversation. Allow your heart to feel while your mind listens. Allow your mind to reason while in tune with your heart. When your heart senses freedom, call forth a word, a picture, a description, or a story that captures the truth that enabled that feeling of freedom.

REFLECTION

REFLECTION

DAY 25 - CONSCIENCE

CONTEMPLATION

The conscience is the voice of the soul. The conscience is the "inner man." The inner man processes through thought, feeling, or a combination of the two. Depending on what governs the mind and heart will indicate whether the conscience can be trusted.

Through practicing *In Spirit* living, we experience a change in the conscience. As the mind and heart begin to transform in the Image of God, over time, the conscience becomes an avenue through which we can hear God's voice. This occurs as "the inner man", in fellowship with God, reflects God's voice. This voice will always contain wisdom, understanding, and the fruit of the Spirit.

A seared conscience lacks feeling. A heart may have a desire that the law of the mind is against. Without love, the mind judges the heart; in return, the heart begins to hate the mind. The heart is going in one direction, the mind in another. In this case, the conscience becomes seared, lacking the voice of the heart. Recognize that a seared conscience voices only the voice of sin controlling the mind being empowered by law.

In Spirit, we engage an understanding God of love through Jesus Christ. *In Spirit*, the mind is fed understanding. The God of love engages the mind to stop judging and start caring for the heart. The heart then begins to love the mind. The mind and heart begin to harmonize to produce wisdom, deepen understanding, and bear fruit of the Spirit. Our conscience now can be trusted.

The Spirit guides us using our trusted conscience. We may experience new convictions. Activities that we participate in may become questionable. On the flip side, you may experience freedom to participate in activities that you once thought wrong.

It is important to keep a clear trusted conscience. This means a conscience that feels no guilt. Going against our conscience severs our mind – heart love bond. If we continue to violate our conscience, we will return to our old way of living and may feel worse than it felt before we experienced *in Spirit* living.

PRACTICE

Find a comfortable, quiet place.

Read Psalm 40 out loud.

Write down any word that captured your attention.

Read Psalm 40 out loud a second time.

Using the word you wrote, structure a sentence.

Read Psalm 40 out loud a third time.

Be still for at least three minutes. Focus on breathing.

Voice a prayer to God using the word and sentence you formed.

Repeat this prayer at least three times.

Throughout the day reflect on Psalm 40.

REFLECTION

Give yourself time to reflect through the day. If you choose, write or draw any reflections you experienced. Explore creativity, perhaps even recording your voice in words or song. This is to allow time for your heart and mind to have a conversation. Allow your heart to feel while your mind listens. Allow your mind to reason while in tune with your heart. When your heart senses freedom, call forth a word, a picture, a description, or a story that captures the truth that enabled that feeling of freedom.

REFLECTION

DAY 26 - SUBCONSCIOUS

CONTEMPLATION

The subconscious holds our underlying instincts. Our subconscious takes control in sudden situations. It, also, controls our actions in one area while our conscious is focused on another.

The subconscious is trainable. The daily conscious effort to pick up an instrument to learn how to play will eventually form an instinct within the subconscious to play the instrument with little conscious effort. Likewise, learning how to ride a bicycle takes conscious effort in the beginning, but, with continual practice, over time becomes part of the subconscious. Through these examples, we come to understand that our subconscious is trained through hearing, seeing, and touching.

Just because we consciously have faith in Christ does not mean our subconscious has been trained to react out of that faith. It takes a considerable amount of faith practice before the subconscious is trained to react according to faith. The subconscious can possess under-lying idols overriding our faith. Training the subconscious can be the key to overcoming a struggle or addiction.

As we live life, we will face sudden trials and circumstances. How we act during these trials, helps us to understand the wellness of our subconscious. Our subconscious actions can easily strike the conscience to cause guilt, or feel shame.

When this occurs, apply the blood of Jesus and acknowledge His life through His Spirit living in you. This will keep you from living in continual guilt or shame. Also, you can use this as a means to identify areas of your soul in which you are weak and seek encouragement from your brothers and sisters reassuring that . . . you are OKAY!

PRACTICE

Idolatry is making God into something He is not. To believe God is somewhere more than He is another could be idolatry. Define and describe other forms of idolatry.

Make a list of religious practices that could promote idolatry to the subconscious. Are there any thought patterns connected to the practice that help promote idolatry to the subconscious?

Are there any practices and thought patterns outside religion that promote idolatry to the subconscious?

Find a comfortable, quiet place.

Be still for at least three minutes. Focus on breathing.

Acknowledge that the Father, Jesus, and Holy Spirit are living in you.

Voice: "Lord, I know You are in the process of making all things new within me. Grant me grace and peace as we journey together in this process. Make me new, Lord. Make me new."
(*repeat three times*)

REFLECTION

Give yourself time to reflect through the day. If you choose, write or draw any reflections you experienced. Explore creativity, perhaps even recording your voice in words or song. This is to allow time for your heart and mind to have a conversation. Allow your heart to feel while your mind listens. Allow your mind to reason while in tune with your heart. When your heart senses freedom, call forth a word, a picture, a description, or a story that captures the truth that enabled that feeling of freedom.

REFLECTION

DAY 27 – BODY AND SOUL CYCLES

CONTEMPLATION

The earth cycles around the sun and the moon cycles around the earth. Through these we experience cycles of the seasons. These cycles affect life on earth in such a way that a dog will begin to grow a heavy coat of fur for the winter and shed it in the summer. Tree leaves fall and spring to life. Birds fly south, then north.

The human body and soul find their habitat in cycles. There are daily, weekly, monthly, and yearly cycles. Once habits are formed within these cycles, the body and soul will develop a rhythm to perform through the cycles.

When my soul (my mind and my heart) experiences a season of tranquility, suddenly I can have a thought or a feeling that causes a shake (a temptation). I often have asked the questions: Why am I feeling this way? or, Why am I thinking this way? Along with this, I sense an urge to do what I feel or think, but truly do not want to do.

Though I may have had a period of "sobriety", these "out of the blue" urges can catch me off guard. What I have sensed is that there maybe a possibility that they come from my body or soul attempting to repeat a cycle from an action, a feeling, or a thought from yesterday, last month, last year, or from a period of years ago (perhaps 3, 7, 10, or 50 years).

Being mindful of my past and understanding the rhythm of my body and soul through cycles helps me to daily prepare for sudden, unwanted urges and helps me to separate who I truly have become from my old way of living, when I experience a "shake."

An event that causes a sudden discomfort can produce an unwanted body or soul cycle. Some triggering events can be the loss of a loved one through death or them leaving (abandonment), divorce, robbery, rape, child abuse, job loss, being wrongly accused for a crime, vehicle wrecks, hunting accidents, terrorist attacks, wars, natural disasters, house fires (especially with loss of emotional attachments).

Repeated actions that produce a temporary feeling of comfort can produce an unwanted body cycle. For example: drinking, smoking, use of drugs, sex, pornography, masturbation, overeating, stealing, lying, gossiping, manipulating, self-isolating, self-pity, gambling, fighting, killing, etc. These actions could have begun as a way to provide comfort after feeling a surge of discomfort from a sudden emotional change.

Over time, these cycles can become so tangled up with each other that we can feel lost (as it affects the heart) and exhausted (as it affects the mind) from the hurt we feel within ourselves, as well as seeing the hurt afflicted on others. *In Spirit* living aids in the untangling and breaking of the unwanted body and soul cycles, caring for the body, bringing healing to the heart and mind, and strengthening relationships. However, this takes time.

The Spirit may guide you to people that can help you through thought and emotional patterns that were prompt by a traumatic event. He may guide you to recognize triggers such as sounds, smells, colors, touch, or sights. Remember God's love for you is unfailing . . . no matter what.

PRACTICE

Find a comfortable, quiet place.

Be still for at least 3 minutes. Focus on breathing.

Acknowledge the presence of the Father, the Son, and the Holy Spirit.

Breath in. He is in you. Breath out. You are in Him.
(repeat three times)

Give praise and thanks to God for His nature of love.

Voice: "But God demonstrates His own love for us in this: While we were still sinners, Christ died for us." (Romans 5:8 NIV)
(repeat three times)

Have you experienced any sudden "shakes?" Have you discovered a cycle in which they occur? Are you aware of what began the cycle?

If the Spirit guides you, share this with at least two others whom you have grown to trust and who have shown unconditional love toward you. Share with them your growth through being *in Spirit*. Allow them to share with you their story.

PRACTICE

Read 1 Peter.

Voice: "Lord Jesus, I know You understand how I feel. Fix my eyes on You in the midst of repeated trials. Fill me with the comfort of Your Holy Spirit, and may I feel the fruit of Your presence: Love, Joy, Peace, Patience, Kindness, Gentleness, Faithfulness, Goodness, and Self-Control, that only You can provide. May this be my eternal source of comfort."
(*repeat three times*)

Keep your friends close, and continue to share with them.

Be patient with yourself, showering yourself with mercy while protecting your soul (heart and mind) from deceit. Continuously giving the body over to participate in actions that provide only temporary comfort keeps the soul from experiencing full eternal comfort available from the Spirit, and can lead to a torn soul where the mind judges the heart, and the heart hates the mind.

REFLECTION

Give yourself time to reflect through the day. If you choose, write or draw any reflections you experienced. Explore creativity, perhaps even recording your voice in words or song. This is to allow time for your heart and mind to have a conversation. Allow your heart to feel while your mind listens. Allow your mind to reason while in tune with your heart. When your heart senses freedom, call forth a word, a picture, a description, or a story that captures the truth that enabled that feeling of freedom.

REFLECTION

DAY 28 - THE INNER GARDEN

CONTEMPLATION

During Jesus' life on earth, He spoke in many parables concerning the kingdom of God. Jesus once said the kingdom of God was among and within us (Luke 17:20-21). As we hear the parable of the sower, let's approach this story as if it were happening within ourselves.

The parable of the sower, found in Matthew 13 and Luke 8, illustrates how seed capable of producing life, being scattered, falls on different types of soil. The different soils are described as being along the path, in rocky places, among thorns, and in good soil. Seed that falls on the good soil produces the crop, while seed falling on the other types of soil encounters an environment that does not cater to producing.

Jesus gives meaning to what this parable means and gives definition to the types of soil that can be found within the heart. He says the seed is the Word of God. This is more than just written words on pages of the Bible. The Word is Jesus, Himself, as well as the words He spoke through all the apostles and prophets. The seed (the Word of God) penetrates the heart through hearing, seeing, and touching.

The path is hard by being walked upon. Seed scattered along the path will only lay on the surface in clear view of the hungry birds. Experiences in life can make the heart hard and, over time, prideful. Pride will keep the Word of God from taking root in the heart.

Though one hears and sees the Word, one will not be able to listen and understand while pride is ruling the heart. Pride is the devil's way of keeping the seed from taking root. The devil makes use of many ways in order to harden our hearts and keep us prideful. Understanding these ways will help soften any soil along the path within the heart.

Other aspects of life that will keep Jesus from yielding His crops within our hearts include troubles, persecution, worry, and love of money. The good news is that Jesus always scatters His seed. He watches to see that His word produces a crop. Any area of our hearts that does not yield the crop, Jesus is ready to cultivate alongside us.

In Spirit takes us to the inner garden. The inner garden is located within your heart where the Word is producing the crop. Search for the inner garden, enter, and stay therein. Within the inner garden is where we find the strength to participate in cultivating the other types of soil. Always remain within the garden. As the garden grows, the soil types will reveal themselves. We do not have to go out searching for them.

PRACTICE

Read Matthew 13 or Luke 8.

Make a list of the illustrations within the parable to their meaning.

Self-examine your heart.

What questions need to be asked to better understand the kingdom?

How does trouble and persecution produce fear in you?

What worries challenges your faith?

Does having wealth or the lack of wealth have any influence on your faith? How so?

Did the apostles understand the kingdom?

Did the apostles ever fall away because of fear?

Did the apostles ever worry?

Were the apostles ever influenced by wealth?

PRACTICE

Find a comfortable, quiet place.

Be still for at least three minutes. Focus on breathing.

Acknowledge that the Father, Jesus, and the Holy Spirit are living in you.

Voice: "Lord, my heart is the new earth possessing different soils. I know there is a garden within my heart, consisting of the good soil that has been cultivated by You where I can feel safe with Your eternal inner presence. Lord, guide me to this place and give me eternal rest in You. Lord, let us work together to grow this garden to encompass my entire heart. In Jesus' Name, AMEN."
(*repeat three times*)

Today's practice is to remain in this garden and to work out from the garden. Identify the different soil types. Cultivate the soil, while *in Spirit*, softening the soil and removing the rocks and thorns. Allow the scattering of seed continually to take place. Be mindful of its growth. Always work outward from within the inner garden of your heart.

REFLECTION

Give yourself time to reflect through the day. If you choose, write or draw any reflections you experienced. Explore creativity, perhaps even recording your voice in words or song. This is to allow time for your heart and mind to have a conversation. Allow your heart to feel while your mind listens. Allow your mind to reason while in tune with your heart. When your heart senses freedom, call forth a word, a picture, a description, or a story that captures the truth that enabled that feeling of freedom.

REFLECTION

REFLECTION

About the Author

TIM MEHTA is the founder and director of In Spirit Rhythm, LLC. He is a graduate of the University of Kentucky with a BS in Mechanical Engineering. He is also a graduate of the Sunset International Bible Institute in Lubbock, Texas, where he received intensive biblical training.

Tim is active in several ministries that lead him to serve in orphanages, sex trafficking rescue centers, and drug and alcohol rehabilitation centers. His heart for healing and his resolve to help restore people's self-respect and self-love are a direct result of overcoming his personal faith crisis.

Tim currently travels throughout the United States and abroad guiding groups of people to a higher spiritual state of love and acceptance. He particularly enjoys the small group and individual conversations that result. He believes the one-on-one experience to be the most powerful and effective way to connect with others on an emotional and spiritual level.

Tim's meditations have led him to be a painter of spiritual imagery. He has created numerous paintings inspired by the meditations he has practiced, and by listening to the divine guidance from within.

Tim currently makes his home in Nashville, Tennessee.

Made in the USA
Coppell, TX
20 November 2020